Bauhaus philosophy
:, craft, and
quality goods,
gs of which we
zing our design
unds, our goal
able, beautiful,
decorative
yn and Jerome

EVELYN AND JEROME ACKERMAN

EVELYN AND JEROME ACKERMAN

CALIFORNIA MID-CENTURY DESIGNERS

LAURA ACKERMAN-SHAW

CONTRIBUTORS
GLENN ADAMSON / DANIELLE CHARLAP
DALE CAROLYN GLUCKMAN / JEFFREY HEAD
DAVID A. KEEPS / JO LAURIA

PRINCIPAL PHOTOGRAPHY
DAN CHAVKIN

POINTED LEAF PRESS

TEACHERS
Gregson

Skrip
SHEAFFER'S

CONTENTS

Part I
Evelyn and Jerome

GROWING UP ACKERMAN

LAURA ACKERMAN-SHAW

"Your house is weird," declared my friends in 1970. Their homes—assemblages of aqua shag carpet, harvest-gold kitchens, and brown vinyl recliners—did not look like mine. Most 10-year-olds definitely did not live with Wegner, Eames, Nelson, Aalto, and Saarinen furniture. An eclectic mix of art and artifacts, curated by my parents, Jerome and Evelyn Ackerman, filled our home. Rya, Navajo, and kilim rugs were scattered across the hardwood floor. Folk art, kachinas, African masks, *Santos* figures, antiques, and art books perched on Japanese *tansus* and Omni shelves. Weaving through the rooms were my parents' paintings, ceramics, and sculpture. Mom's Panelcarve designs accented walls. Dad's hardware bejeweled cabinetry. Outside, Architectural Pottery sprouted jade plants in our backyard.

In my Scandinavian-furnished room, two hangings decorated the walls over my bed. A large appliqué, "The House That Love Built," displayed finger puppets Mom had made for me. A dozen of them ultimately became kits for my preschool fundraiser, garnering awards and press. Above my head hung Mom's whimsical *Garden* wall hanging. A Steelcase (in my mind "architect desk") established residency under my window.

My parents bought our modest tract house in Culver City, California, in 1956 from my uncle Milton. They added a large light-filled studio with floor-to-ceiling fireplace and terra-cotta tile floors designed by the architect Emiel Becksy, a friend from Craig Ellwood's office. On one side was Mom's handmade drafting table; on the other, wood doors set atop filing cabinets served as counters for a dry-mount press, large paper cutter, overhead projector, and Elna sewing machine. Certainly nobody I knew had not one but two studios (the smaller one doubled as a dark room while I was in high school).

Unlike me, my parents did not grow up in artistic homes. Instead of crayons, I used pastels, colored pencils, and X-Acto knives (eliciting dire safety warnings). Mom and I would stop at The Egg and The Eye gallery (the founder Edith Wyle and the buyer Dorothy Garwood were friends) on the way to a Los Angeles County Museum of Art class or La Brea Tar Pits excavation. An only child, I learned about good design by osmosis, exposed to artists, architects, designers, and curators. I read publications such as the *Los Angeles Times Home* magazine (that featured my parents' work so often, people asked if they were on the payroll), *Graphis*, *Interiors*, and *Sunset*. I accompanied them to museum exhibitions, where I was instructed to select my favorite piece based not on notoriety, but on what I liked.

Dad smoked a pipe, Mom wore Marimekko—I thought they were very sophisticated. Devoted parents, Evy and Jerry (as they were known), maintained deep friendships for decades, respected for their warmth, authenticity, humor, intelligence, generosity, and kindness. Their artist friendships stretched back to university days including with the well-known ceramists Ka Kwong Hui and Fong Chow, with whom they became close at Alfred University.

A born entertainer, Dad loved music. His family could not afford piano lessons, so he never learned to read music, and voice lessons for his lyric baritone were cut short by World War II. He loved big bands, Nat King Cole, Billie Holiday, and Sinatra. I can still hear him singing "Begin the Beguine" and "All or Nothing at All." I danced on his feet, laughing, while he imitated Fats Waller, singing about "pedal extremities" and "your feet's too big." His signature humor imbued stories and songs he wrote for me.

Dad was also a storyteller extraordinaire. Articulate and witty, he recounted his life experiences in colorful, evocative tales. When he described meeting Mom, it was a movie set replete with shimmering fabrics and roaring fire. He retold his time at Rhein-Main Air Base as a control tower operator where where roving bands of young men called "werewolves" threatened 24-hour shifts in the "bitch box." His solution was to trade cigarettes for an Airedale Terrier, who he named Schnapps and carried up the 40-foot ladder each shift. On their honeymoon, my parents found one of their hotels booked, so Dad called from a phone booth across the street masquerading as "Mr. Ackerman's secretary"—needless to say, he got a room. He shared being a tour guide for Wilhelm Kåge of Gustavsberg pottery in Sweden, during a taxi strike in Detroit. A delicate Farsta pot sat above the television, a gift from Wilhelm; a letter from his wife Gabrielle thanking Dad for his oil painting accompanied a set of Gense flatware we used daily. I can picture Dad and Peter Voulkos with their contrasting heights sitting on the back step of his apartment drinking wine and discussing ceramics shows they juried together.

Mom was scholarly but shy. An exemplary student, she received an MFA honors scholarship at Wayne University. In college she discovered German Expressionists, Modigliani, Cézanne, Matisse, Klee, and Rembrandt. She treasured books. As an undergraduate in the 1940s she saved for a year to buy Al Hirschfeld's book *Harlem*, a limited-edition folio with color lithographs. She gave me beautifully illustrated books such as Maurice Sendak's *Where the Wild Things Are*. For my eighth birthday, she took me to Zeitlin & Ver Brugge, her favorite antiquarian bookstore, to buy me an Audubon print.

Mom let me use her drafting table, where perched on her high swivel chair, I would fish in a cigar box that she had covered in Japanese rice paper to find just the right Prismacolor pencil. She saved all my drawings and made fanciful hand-stamped boxes in which to store them, my name embroidered on the flap of each. At my elementary school she was the

OPPOSITE Archie, a miniature poodle, joined Jerry, Evelyn, and Laura in a happy family portrait in 1964 outside of the Ackermans' Culver City home.

library committee chair and created bookplates and display cases illustrating exotic and fanciful tales. She taught me how to make a cloisonné, how to compose a photograph, and insisted that I take typing because it was a useful skill.

For my sixth birthday, my parents wrote and performed a play (Dad made a stage, Mom crafted puppets), while my friends and I sat enraptured on the floor of the studio. Mom adored puppets, and subsequent birthday parties were often at the Bob Baker Marionette Theater. A skilled seamstress, she made dolls, stuffed animals, and numerous Halloween costumes. When she stopped smoking in 1964 she distracted herself by making a dollhouse for me complete with needlepoint rugs and handmade ceramic tiles. Using my drawings, she embroidered a miniature bedspread. That project led her to become an antique doll and toy collector and an internationally respected authority and author. She took me to antiques shows where I learned that it was not only important to know what you were buying, but also to recognize quality and craftsmanship. She always gravitated to textiles and appropriately volunteered as a researcher specializing in 18th-century fashion in the Costume and Textile department at the Los Angeles County Museum of Art.

In kindergarten, I begged my parents for a Newfoundland—the largest breed of dog I knew. My parents were, unsurprisingly, not in favor. When they eventually succumbed, I got a much smaller puppy, who I named Archie. After we picked him up, I skipped into Dad's showroom office, all Keds and curls, with a little grey bundle and thought I could never be happier than in that moment.

Unless Mom was helping in the showroom, she usually worked at home so she could be with me. Incredibly focused, she immersed herself intensely in each project. For every design they produced, she had sketched many more. In April 1961, the *Los Angeles Times Home* magazine claimed that "so many types of decorative art bear the signature of Evelyn Ackerman that one might think it were a firm name with a stableful of designers behind it." She was an extraordinary researcher, filling file cabinets with ideas and inspiration. In 1955 five years before I was born, Disneyland, the optimistic epitome of California, opened. The next year *Craft Horizons* published a special issue on California, proclaiming, "Bright colors seem brighter and warm colors warmer in that brilliant saturation of sunlight." My parents were included in that issue. The jubilant shades of many of Mom's designs were not only a reflection of that time but of her unerring eye for color.

At the heart of my parents' narrative is an unwavering love story—for each other, for me, for design. Their personal and professional lives intertwined, and their 64-year love affair resulted in a rare artistic and entrepreneurial partnership that produced a prolific and diverse body of work. In 1963 *West Coast Sourcebook* talked about their company and roles: "In the case of ERA's designer-owners, who work so closely together, it is proper to speak of a single career." While their personalities were very different—Mom was quiet and introverted, Dad gregarious and extroverted—they shared a deep commitment to each other and to their work. Mom laughed that few people could work together for so many years and survive, let alone thrive; Dad teased that it was a "trial marriage."

True partners, my parents collaborated closely while drawing upon distinct artistic visions. A deep mutual respect for each other's abilities allowed them to meld their talents. Often with design couples of this time, the husband was front and center, but in my parents' case it was the opposite—Mom was the lead designer. But everything they created was done in partnership; no design was produced without agreeing that it met their aesthetic standards and a commercial need. They reviewed colors, media, and sizes, and Dad, who had a product-design bent, often determined the best way to produce a design.

Despite their international business and personal relationships, my parents did not travel much. Mom hated flying and regretfully we never traveled to the craft workshops in Mexico, Japan, Italy, or other countries. Occasionally we visited family in Detroit, where we were regarded as California bohemians. For most family vacations (often coupled with business), we piled into our station wagon to Palm Springs, San Diego, San Francisco, or Idyllwild. My favorite was Dad's self-described "beach bum" getaway: a rented house on Malibu beach.

In 1964 the ERA showroom moved to Beverly Boulevard in the Robertson design district. On my own, I was allowed to visit Jules Seltzer (where Dad sold his first Jenev order), Herman Miller, and Knoll a few doors down. I loved sitting in Dad's office while he conducted business on the phone—he was always doodling, and I would sit across his desk with my pencil and paper and pretend to be him. I was less fond of the showroom's sisal carpet, installed before it was chic, because it hurt my bare feet. While my friends toiled at Winchell's Donut House or Baskin-Robbins, I graduated from stuffing catalogs in envelopes to packing orders in the warehouse to assisting interior designers in the showroom and buyers at trade shows. "To the trade," "FOB," "out on memo" were part of my lexicon. It never occurred to me that a typical childhood did not include accompanying one's dad to architectural offices, taking international visitors to Disneyland, or seeing one's parents' designs in banks and restaurants.

Looking back now, it is not just their artistic talent that stands out. Exceptionally entrepreneurial, they also embodied an incredible work ethic. The fact that they uprooted themselves from Detroit to move to Los Angeles, stretched beyond the boundaries of their education, built a business from scratch, and created a lasting body of work is an amazing achievement. My parents worked a lot, but always made time for me.

I experienced the business firsthand—the effort required to manage marketing, sales, displays,

OPPOSITE When Laura was three years old, Evelyn sketched a quick portrait of her daughter wearing her favorite red hat. OVERLEAF LEFT In the studio, Evelyn developed most of her designs at a walnut drafting table that had been handmade for her in the late 1940s by a friend, the architect Eugene Alexander, who later worked for George Nelson. OVERLEAF RIGHT The whimsical 23-by-45-inch *Cat and Bird* wool tapestry, woven in Italy and later produced in Mexico, hung in the entry foyer of the Ackermans' California home and features strong colors and simplified naturalistic forms.

Sesto Meucci
OF FLORENCE

suppliers, and inventory. Given the breadth and depth of products, people thought ERA Industries was a large company. In reality, it was a small operation with a few employees (warehouseman, bookkeeper, showroom manager) and independent sales representatives for national coverage in the contract furnishings and interior design market. Without a large company like a Herman Miller to support manufacturing, marketing, and distribution, my parents handled all aspects of the business themselves. They operated with honesty and integrity, and they seemed to know everyone in the design field. Long before it was a buzzword, they ethically sourced production around the world, working with the same families for generations.

I saw how challenging it was not only to design a product, but also to produce, market, and sell it. Each design was hand drawn and sent with detailed instructions, for surface treatment and color. With paper taped to a wall in the studio, Mom laid a tissue or an acetate of a small drawing on the overhead projector to trace a full-sized template. She was meticulous. The smell of wood at A&M Woodcarving when I joined them to review masters and the roar of jets at LAX when I accompanied Dad to pick up shipments at customs are vivid memories. Business was conducted via letters (many requiring translation) or the occasional expensive international telephone call. My parents embraced experimentation in techniques and materials for creative and scalable production solutions, but bringing a product to market was labor-intensive—especially in the days before computers, fax, email, FedEx, or cell phones. The constant demand to produce new designs every six months for Los Angeles Gift Shows (first at the Ambassador and Biltmore hotels, followed by the Convention Center) and trade shows required that a design be completed, from concept to finished product, in a tight timeframe.

Because products were added frequently and costs changed, Mom typed the pricelists, first on a Royal Manual, eventually on an IBM Selectric, which I used to type many a high school report. They drew elevations, provided typesetter specifications, and pasted up ads and brochures themselves. Mom painstakingly placed type and cut Rubylith over photographs glued to board with instructions for the printers. Dad supervised photo shoots. Always in search of other products to complement ERA offerings, my parents consulted international trade journals and wrote to consulates from Finland to France, Poland to Peru, Belgium to Brazil, China to Canada.

Problems periodically arose—suppliers went out of business, shipments were late, colors were off, or quality was poor. One weaver wrote in 1963, "I cannot find anyone who [sic] tincture and prepare the wool. Here all the women doing that work are now working in the hotels. I have decided to give up." Even natural catastrophes intervened. Their Florentine hardware agent detailed the 1966 flood: "We are all safe, but our business has been completely destroyed as we were submerged under 12 feet of water, mud, and oil. It is hard to figure out the consequences for our beloved city."

I did not fully appreciate my parents' talents, both as artists and as entrepreneurs, until I was an adult—their curiosity about materials, the global élan of their designs, the influence of their fine-art training, and the tenacity they brought to their careers. Although I spent many hours in the showroom, I wish I had paid better attention to my parents' creative process and business dealings and had asked more questions. I wish, too, that I had taken more art history and design courses during my Stanford education—I felt I did not possess my parents innate artistic talent, so I only dabbled.

Perhaps because of their wide-ranging styles and media, my parents' work remained under the radar until the early 2000s. They were surprised and delighted to see it appreciated, its timeless quality transcending mid-century modern—a term that did not exist when they worked as designer-craftsmen. This resurgence of interest led to museum exhibitions and press. I nominated them for distinguished alumni awards at their alma maters and watched them, at age 90 and 86, proudly don caps and gowns to lead the Wayne State University graduation procession. Alfred recognized Dad in 2010 as well, and in honor of his centennial, I endowed the Evelyn and Jerome Ackerman Scholarship at Wayne State University and the Jerome Ackerman Internship at the Alfred Ceramic Art Museum, both for undergraduate art students.

Like many children of well-known designers, it took me years to recognize their contributions. It never occurred to me that growing up Ackerman was special; I took for granted what I perceived as a normal childhood. Ironically, I resisted joining the family business, and it was only when I was in my fifties that I fully appreciated my experience and how exemplary my parents were, both as designers and people. I established Ackerman Modern and discovered a role I am passionate about—serving as steward of my parents' design legacy and preserving, protecting, and promoting it. Now when I work with my parents' archives, I view them through the lens of a daughter with a dash of design historian. Reissuing designs has allowed me to stay true to their aesthetics while inviting in new audiences.

Growing up Ackerman affected me in profound ways that I did not recognize for many years. Now I truly appreciate how extraordinary my parents were in all aspects of their life, marriage, and work and how lucky I was to be their daughter.

OPPOSITE Jerry took the photograph, wrote the accompanying copy, and designed the advertisement for the trade magazine *Interiors* in 1963 for the Ackermans' ERA company. It humorously depicts his daughter, Laura, the budding artist.

LAURA ACKERMAN, HEAD OF DESIGN RESEARCH, DEPT. OF YOUNG IDEAS.

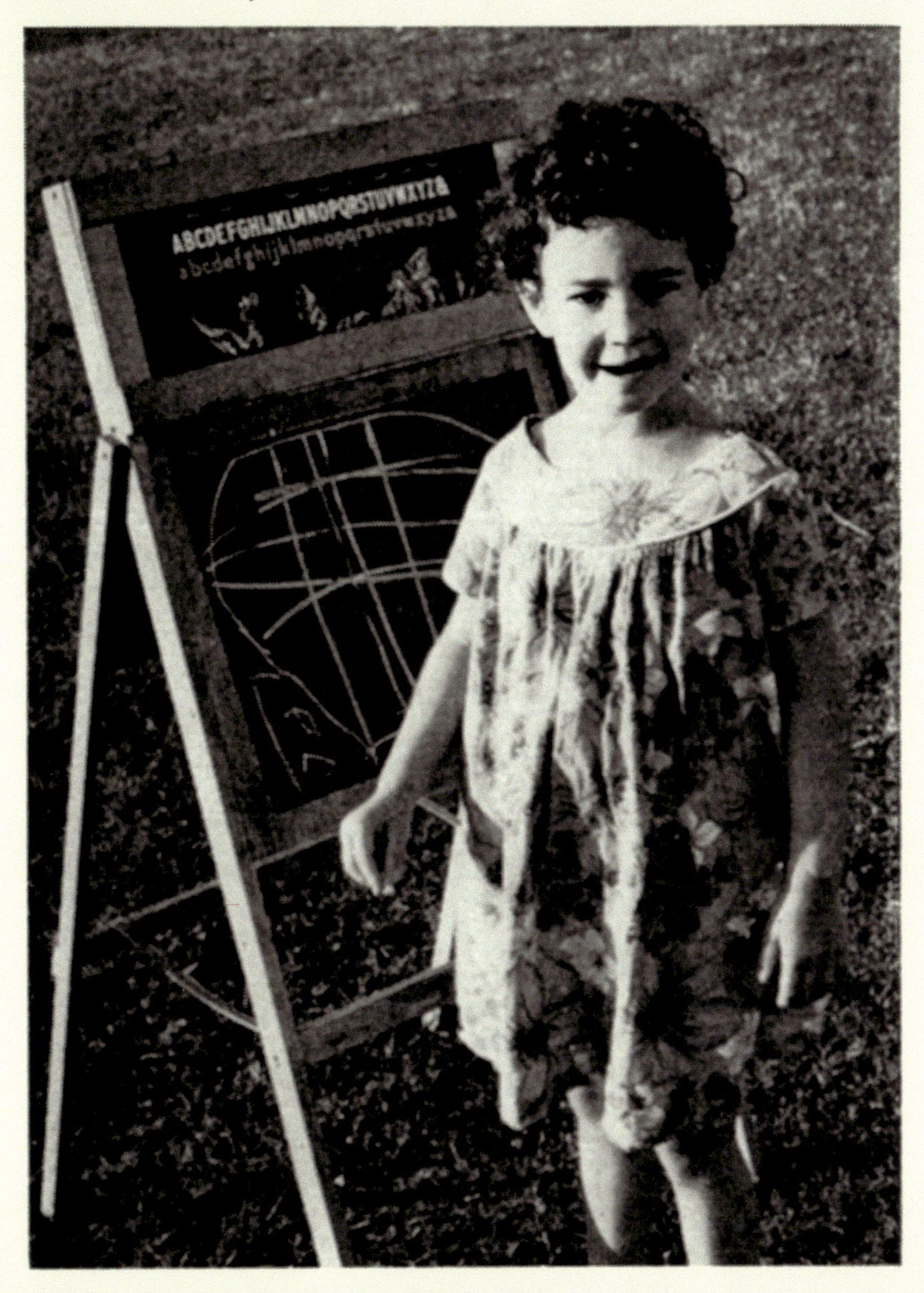

ERA

8703 MELROSE AVE., LOS ANGELES 69, CALIF.

MULTIPLE CHOICE: THE INTERDISCIPLINARY ACKERMANS

GLENN ADAMSON

Just when you think you know the story of American design, it turns around and surprises you all over again. Certainly, this is true of any encounter with the wonderful work of Jerome (Jerry) and Evelyn Ackerman. They were among the most prolific artist couples of the 20th century, and once upon a time, their reputation preceded them. Included in every edition of the influential *California Design* survey exhibitions, which stretched from 1954 to the bicentennial year of 1976, they were West Coast craft royalty, the modest king and queen of a middle-class realm. Since then, as is the way with designers (particularly those whose works are so finely calibrated to their own times), they have become rather less well-known than they should be. The book you hold in your hands is a welcome opportunity to rediscover their artistry. It is a story full of amazements.

What is surprising about the Ackermans is not so much the quality of their work or even their imaginativeness. Those acquainted with the golden age of the craft movement—from 1945 to about 1980—will know well the extraordinary number of makers (hundreds, probably) who somehow rose to a similar standard. What astonishes, rather, is the sheer range of Jerry and Evelyn Ackerman's output. They made ceramics, textiles, enamels, woodcarvings, metalwork, mosaics, toys, sculpture, silk screens, and paintings. Perhaps above all, they were graphic designers of a kind, ones blessed with the rare ability to translate their ideas into seemingly any material they chose.

What is more, the Ackermans experimented with many different means of organizing their production, across a spectrum from one-off commissions to quasi–mass production. Sometimes they used methods like slip casting and machine-assisted carving for the purposes of efficiency. In the majority of cases, their products were made entirely by hand, just not their own. The Ackermans were both highly skilled, but they realized that if they fabricated everything themselves, their prices would be quite high and their output small, limiting them to an exclusive market. They wanted to sell well-designed products to people like themselves, people without much disposable income. So instead of doing what they loved most—making things—they devoted much of their time to the business of craft, sending design drawings, detailed instructions, and material samples to a global network of artisans, with Jerry serving as a product developer, marketer, and salesman.

The Ackermans' strategy of far-flung craft sourcing began in 1957 when they had their first mosaics fabricated in Mexico. They made this move somewhat reluctantly; as Jerry later said, "We wanted the satisfaction of doing every step in the production, since our backgrounds were so strongly steeped in the handcraft tradition." Given this orientation, though, Mexico was a logical place to start; it was not only close at hand, but also extraordinarily rich in artisanal history and capability. In forging connections there, the Ackermans were following in the footsteps of other craft luminaries of the time, such as Anni Albers, Sheila Hicks, and Cynthia Sargent. Unlike these other figures, however, they actually set up sustainable business relationships south of the border.

After getting their mosaic operation going, the Ackermans started having weavings made in Mexico, too; also in Italy, where they had their hardware cast; Greece, where women made needlepoint for them; India, where they worked with a group of embroiderers; and Japan, where craftspersons normally specializing in producing hooked rugs (at a time when the economy was still recovering from the war, comparatively affordable) made them wall hangings. Notably, the majority of the artisans they employed were women, for whom the orders received from Jerry and Evelyn were an important source of livelihood.

These collaborations were quite innovative for the time, anticipating the work of contemporary designers including Stephen Burks and Patricia Urquiola, who have similarly embraced global artisanship as a means of empowering their own creativity. Yet the Ackermans' entrepreneurial approach did also fit into a broader current. There was a strong sense of internationalism in the craft movement, which had gotten its start during the war under the leadership of Aileen Osborn Webb. Already in the early 1950s, the magazine of the American Craftsmen's Council, *Craft Horizons*, had become amazingly adventurous in its coverage —an artisanal equivalent to *National Geographic*. The Ackermans were regularly featured in its pages. They also showed at the Council's New York City headquarters, the Museum of Contemporary Crafts, including in its 1956 inaugural exhibition, *Craftsmanship in a Changing World* (Jerome was represented by two ceramics, Evelyn by a felt appliqué and a mosaic wall panel).

In 1964 Webb founded the World Crafts Council with the goal of fostering mutually beneficial exchange across borders. Concurrently, designers such as Alexander Girard and Charles and Ray Eames (acknowledged role models for Jerry and Evelyn) were avidly collecting folk objects from abroad. Department stores were importing high-quality handmade goods—yet another activity that the Ackermans pursued as an extension of their studio practice. In their showroom, examples of their own work appeared alongside items gathered from near and far: Scandinavia, Latin America, and Africa as well as from across the

OPPOSITE As a freshman at the University of Michigan, Evelyn took one weaving class and experimented with different yarns, as shown in this runner. OVERLEAF Working on a mosaic table in 1956, Evelyn carefully cut Italian glass tiles and applied them to a wood backing. She executed all the mosaic work herself until the Ackermans set up a workshop to meet demand. *Warrior King* aluminum castings and Jenev vases filled the small work area. PAGES 28–29 Evelyn snapped this photograph of Jerry with some of his ceramics at Stony Brook near the Alfred University campus in 1951.

United States. It was a unified view of design, at once cosmopolitan and unpretentious.

The Ackermans were equally encompassing in their design sources, drawing on everything from East Asian ceramics (which Jerry had studied at Wayne University and Alfred University) to Byzantine mosaics, ancient Mesoamerican stone carvings, and contemporaneous Native American art. Their inspirations from these diverse traditions were always respectful, even graceful, never stepping into the direct appropriation of cultural motifs. While always interested in other people's art, their own aesthetic sensibility was too strong to be subsumed into any one influence. Jerry said that "Evy had such a wide, expansive art history touching on so many different areas and arenas, that it wasn't difficult for her. She just had to have something to spark her to get going."

Remarkably, given the breadth of their horizons, the Ackermans also helped to define the local California look. The *Los Angeles Times* in 1951 characterized the style as having "glowing color, originality of treatment, and simplicity of design"—an absolutely apt description of the Ackermans' work. It comes as no surprise that they were featured (and also advertised) in John Entenza's *Arts & Architecture* magazine, that defining publication of California modernism, or that their work found its way into the Case Study Houses that were prime experimental platforms for the emergent idiom. Like so many other California designers, they were also adept at keeping up with the trends, shifting their palette, and exploring new artistic directions as they emerged, such as Op and Pop Art. They kept adopting new techniques, making it look easy. It is striking how often they executed similar designs in more than one medium—as if devising a motif were the hard thing and rendering it in weaving or mosaic were the simple part. In fact, ideas flowed from Evelyn's pen as easily as string quartets did from Haydn's; their interdisciplinarity was not motivated by pragmatism. It was, rather, a matter of curiosity: What will *this* look like if we have it made like *that*?

This is, of course, the essential question of craft; if efficiency were all that counted, it could easily be accomplished through machine production. Again, the Ackermans were keenly aware of this dimension of their work. "We feel that craftsmen living in a machine age have a bigger job than ever," Evelyn told the *Detroit News* in 1955. "After all, a machine-made article is no better than the artist who designed it." Accordingly, their approach to every craft in their ever-enlarging repertoire always foregrounded its special attributes. As Evelyn made clear, design was not just an unconstrained space of visualization —it had to respect the demands of technique, treating the apparent limits of a given medium as a creative parameter.

The weavers they worked with in Mexico, for example, typically made serapes on simple flat looms; it would have been extremely difficult for them to execute complex figuration, as might be possible using a tapestry technique or a more complicated Jacquard loom. The Ackermans counted on the natural variation of hand-dyed yarns to achieve a lively visual effect. Similarly, in Evelyn's correspondence with fabricator A&M Woodcarving, she requested that tool marks be left on the surface rather than polished away, even if this seemed somewhat crude in detail. "Use your judgment," she added encouragingly, "letting the carving machine needs guide you."

In the aggregate, these decisions resulted in what the British craft theorist David Pye called "diversity"—the humanizing effect of a subtle, infinitely variegated surface. This quality of complicated nuance in the Ackermans' work, in combination with the simple charm of their iconography, lent great warmth to the modern interior. Alongside other leading protagonists of the California design movement—the furniture maker Sam Maloof, the ceramic designer Edith Heath, and the potters Otto and Gertrud Natzler—they showed that handcraft was totally compatible with modernity itself. With sufficient ingenuity, enterprise, and material intelligence, it was possible to infuse tradition with the new and vice versa.

Jerry and Evelyn are no longer with us, and the particular type of sunny, insouciant globalism that they exemplified no longer feels available—so much more acutely aware, as we are, of the complex issues involved in cross-cultural exchange. Yet the optimistic energy that they brought to the wide horizons of craft does feel very much worth holding onto. Faced with the great multiple-choice questions about creative life—deciding which of many mediums to use; whether to use craft or serial production; to work by hand or machine; to explore figuration or abstraction; to see themselves as designers of California, the United States, or the world at large—they came up with their own answer, and in doing so made their indelible mark on design history: "all of the above."

OPPOSITE Decorated with blue Mishima dots, this 5-inch-high stoneware bud vase was shown in 1954 at the Wichita Art Association *National Decorative Arts and Ceramics Exhibition* and in 1955 at the California State Fair and the Detroit Institute of Arts *Michigan Artist-Craftsman* exhibition. OVERLEAF John Entenza's influential *Arts & Architecture* was first art directed by Alvin Lustig then by John Follis. The editorial board was a Who's Who of mid-century architects and designers—many of whom were clients of the Ackermans—including Walter Gropius, Richard Neutra, Welton Becket, Victor Gruen, Marcel Breuer, William Pereira, A. Quincy Jones, Gregory Ain, Craig Ellwood, Isamu Noguchi, Finn Juhl, George Nelson, Dorothy Liebes, Edward Frank, and Harold Grieve. The May 1961 issue highlighted the Ackermans' tapestries and mosaics.

arts & architecture
MAY 1961
FOLLIS

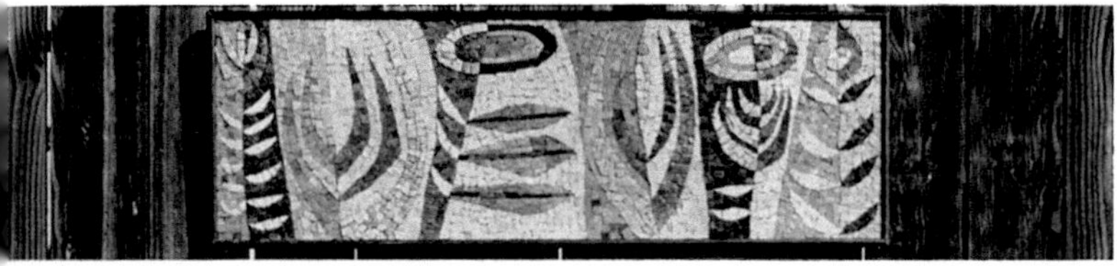

[M]OSAIC, "FLOWER ABSTRACT," 12" X 36"

2

[T]APESTRIES AND MOSAICS BY EVELYN AND [J]EROME ACKERMAN

We show two of the activities of the talented designers who, working in [c]ollaboration, have been active in the design field for many years and [i]n many different media. In most cases, they devote themselves to design[i]ng, using the skills of native craftsmen whenever possible to execute the [f]inal projects.

They have worked with and made important contributions to numerous [a]rchitectural commissions and are certainly among those of the designers [w]hose work is richly imaginative and skillfully conceived.

3

. "FLOWER ABSTRACT," TAPESTRY DESIGNED BY EVELYN ACKERMAN; 20" X 60"

. HANDHOOKED RUG DESIGNED BY EVELYN ACKERMAN, "DIAMONDS," IN YELLOW, ORANGE, TAN, WHITE AND BLACK; 4' X 6'

. "PATHWAY," HANDHOOKED AREA RUG, 4' X 6'; BLUE GREEN ON GREEN; BY EVELYN ACKERMAN

. HANDWOVEN TAPESTRY, "ABSTRACT," 20" X 62", PINK, MAGENTA, RED, YELLOW, BLACK, TURQUOISE AND VIOLET

. "HOT SUMMER LANDSCAPE"; HANDWOVEN TAPESTRY, ALL WOOL; HOT PINK, RED, ORANGE WITH BLUE AND GREEN ACCENTS; 28" X 63"; DESIGNED BY EVELYN ACKERMAN

[M]OSAIC, "AUTUMN ABSTRACT," 12" X 48". COLORS: YELLOW, ORANGE, RED, WHITE, TAN, [B]ROWN

[M]OSAIC, "PENNANT," 12" X 60". COLORS: BLUES, TURQUOISE, GREEN, WHITE

[M]OSAIC, "ELLIPSES," 12" X 60"—AVAILABLE IN WARM AND COOL COLOR SCHEMES. COOL [C]OLORS: WHITE, GRAY, BLUES, GREEN, BLACK. WARM COLORS: ORANGE, YELLOW, TAN, [W]HITE.

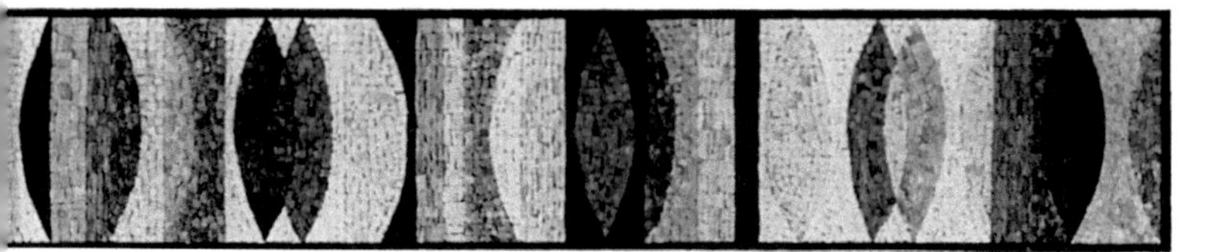

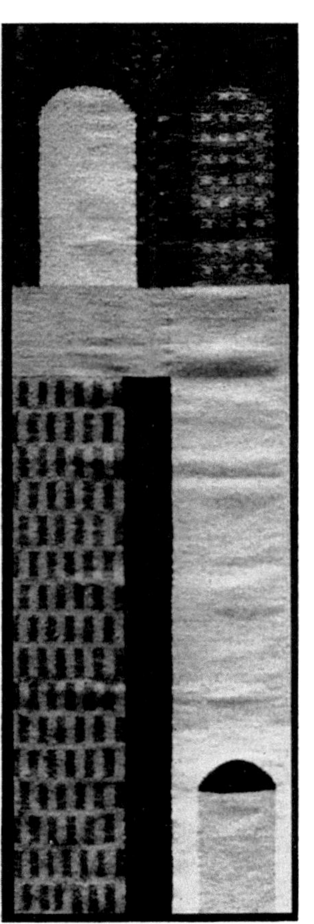

4

5

A LOVE STORY

JEFFREY HEAD

The love story that became Jerry and Evelyn's life together began in 1948 when he was 28 and she was 24. They grew up in the same neighborhood in Depression-era Detroit and attended the same schools (Roosevelt, Durfee, and Central), but never met because of their age difference. Born on January 29, 1920, to Louis Ackerman and Esther Greenberg, Jerry joined brother Bernard, who was 12. Evelyn and her twin sister, Roslyn, were born on January 12, 1924, to Jacob Lipchinsky (the children later changed their last name to Lipton) and Sarah Turetsky, following brothers Leo, Raymond, and Milton.

Growing up, neither was exposed to art, but both loved drawing, even at an early age. Despite their proximity to the Detroit Institute of Arts, their families did not take them to that museum. In 1939, by the time Evelyn was a high school senior, Jerry had begun his art studies at Wayne University (now Wayne State University) as an art major under the National Youth Administration, earning 30 cents an hour to defray his tuition. He left in 1941 to work at the United States Naval Ordnance during World War II, then joined the Air Force and was stationed in Germany at Rhein-Main Air Base as a control tower operator. Enrolled in the University of Michigan, Evelyn returned home when her father died and her brothers enlisted, transferring to Wayne where the art program featured young, talented professors. Ernst Scheyer, one of her art history professors, so inspired Evelyn that she took 11 classes with him. After completing her BFA with distinction, Evelyn pursued her MFA on a scholarship.

In late 1946, after his discharge and a six-month visit to his brother in Los Angeles, Jerry returned to Detroit. In 1948 a friend told Jerry about a beautiful young woman who was working at the Lucé Lipton Interior Design Studio. He dropped in and introduced himself; she reminded him they had met in the Wayne art studio. They talked about their shared interest and he boldly asked her out. Jerry was drawn not only to her beauty but her intelligence. Jerry's personality, humor, and creativity—along with his wonderful singing voice—gave him an advantage over Evelyn's many suitors. They were married later that year and set up their first apartment in Detroit filling it with silk screened drapes, Eames furniture, ethnic art, paintings, and pottery, as Bartók played in the background.

A salesman for his cousin's steel business, Jerry returned to school on his $130-a-month GI Bill. He intended to major in commercial art. Instead he discovered painting and ceramics and took his first ceramics class from John Foster. Both graduated from Wayne in 1950—for Evelyn, a Masters in Fine Arts, and for Jerry, a Bachelors in Science, as he had matriculated to the School of Education in order to receive an art-teaching certificate.

During Jerry's senior year, Charles M. Harder, the chairman of the New York State College of Ceramics at Alfred University was the guest juror of the senior art exhibition at Wayne State where Jerry had both ceramics and oil paintings on display. Impressed by Jerry's ceramics, he invited Jerry into the prestigious graduate program. The Ackermans briefly considered moving to Champaign when Harder recommended Jerry for a position at the University of Illinois, but because he could not afford the airfare, Jerry passed on the opportunity.

Even before completing his MFA at Alfred in 1952, Jerry exhibited in national ceramics shows such as the *Syracuse Ceramic National*, the *Wichita Decorative Arts and Crafts National*, the *Smithsonian Invitational Kiln Club*, and the *Scripps Invitational*. The development of the Ackermans' aesthetic sensibilities, which combined the fine and decorative arts, was taking form in their individual work. It would lead them to a shared vision and an inseparable life together as designers.

For Jerry and Evelyn, the most influential experience was the *For Modern Living* exhibition, curated by Alexander Girard at the Detroit Institute of Arts in 1949. It was the young couple's first exposure to Charles and Ray Eames, George Nelson, Eero Saarinen, Harry Bertoia, Eva Zeisel, Kurt Versen, Stanislav V'Soske, and other designers whose work now defines mid-century modern. The collection of everyday household objects offered the Ackermans a fresh perspective on design as a career and, buoyed by postwar optimism, they were inspired to pursue their dream. They began to see themselves as a unique couple with a singular creative point of view.

With its sunny, mild weather, California was a magnet for creative, independent-minded artists and designers in the early 1950s. Jerry and Evelyn visited Los Angeles and saw the possibilities in the growing housing market, art scene, and economy. They met Beatrice Wood, Gertrud and Otto Natzler, John Follis and Rex Goode, and Joseph Eichler. Worried that they would not be able to make a living, Eichler, a real estate developer, assured them, "I'm building hundreds of houses and you can sell a pot to each one!" They moved to Los Angeles in 1952, becoming a vital part of the creative community and the golden era of California design. Evelyn remembered, "We had very little money, but we had a dream and each other. We worked very hard, but it was easy to because we were in love, and we loved what we were doing."

OPPOSITE The Ackermans celebrated their wedding on September 12, 1948, at Evelyn's mother's house in Detroit. OVERLEAF LEFT The artist Saul Steinberg illustrated the catalog for Alexander Girard's *For Modern Living* exhibition at the Detroit Institute of Arts, which inspired the young couple. OVERLEAF RIGHT The September 1963 California edition of *American Home* magazine featured an Eichler home in Lucas Valley, San Rafael, California, designed by the architect Claude Oakland. The interior design by Matt Kahn, seen through the atrium, glows with gemlike colors reflected in the *Windows* tapestry.

an exhibition

for modern living

THE DETROIT INSTITUTE OF ARTS • DETROIT, MICHIGAN, U. S. A.

ROBERT W. HOUSEMAN

BRIGHTEST LITTLE HOUSE IN THE WEST

he decorating in this beautifully esigned home reminds us of ewels sparkling in a glass showase. Charcoal-colored carpeting nd white painted walls provide clean, subtle setting for the ery, gemlike colors strewn about he living room, seen here viewed rom the rear terrace. Lean, upolstered seating units at right ngles facing the fireplace are a bold modern mosaic of color and pattern. Imaginative lighting adds to the luminous quality of the room.

But the real show-window drama of the house stems from the basic architectural concept. Designed by Claude Oakland, A.I.A. for Eichler Homes in Lucas Valley, San Rafael, California, this American contemporary is built around an open-to-the-sky atrium. Virtually every room shares the airy, leafy charm of the inner court, although the bedrooms are pleasantly cushioned with privacy. The versatile plan encourages tasteful decorating in any style. Turn the page for more about this brilliant modern home with its ancient Roman air of ease and grace.

Los Angeles Times

HOME

MAGAZINE SECTION

JANUARY 22, 1956

William Webb

Pasadena art museum's 2nd annual California design exposition

See Page 11

CALIFORNIA DESIGN EXHIBITIONS

JO LAURIA AND DALE CAROLYN GLUCKMAN

The story of California modernism begins with World War II and the westward migration of Americans searching for jobs in wartime industries. This led to profound economic and demographic changes. People continued to move to California after the war, attracted by economic opportunity and the mild climate. By 1962 California surpassed New York as the most populous state, shifting the regional balance to the West Coast. With the expanding population came freeways, shopping centers, and tract housing.

Notably, the work of high-profile architects was showcased in the *Arts & Architecture* Case Study House program launched in California in 1945 by the publisher John Entenza. As the housing market exploded with the proliferation of modern, suburban homes, the demand for well-designed interior furnishings grew, with a new focus on an indoor-outdoor lifestyle. This resulted in Los Angeles becoming a major center of modernist design.

Furnishing industries, design firms, and craft studios arose, stimulated by this postwar housing boom. The acclaimed industrial designer Henry Dreyfuss was attracted to the "willingness to take a chance on new ideas." From the 1950s to the mid-1970s, the designer-craftsmen of the Golden State were at the center of innovation and individual expression in American applied arts. During this period, the *California Design* program was initiated to showcase groundbreaking works that became the hallmark of California modernism, reflecting a revival of craft and the adaptation of industrial technology to artistic use.

Jerry and Evelyn Ackerman were pioneers in this movement and an integral part of the creative energy of the era. Opening their Los Angeles design studio in 1952, the couple played a central role in shaping a distinctive California decorative style—one characterized by the use of natural materials, textural contrasts, saturated colors, and an experimental approach to form. Their attractive and well-made objects reflected the principles of modern design as defined by the philosophy of the Bauhaus (the influential German art and design school that flourished from 1919 to 1933). The Ackermans built on the Bauhaus belief that the "applied" and "fine" arts were equally important and vital. Over the course of their professional careers, they integrated their knowledge of fine art, craft, and folk art to create a body of iconic work that became emblematic of the California modernist aesthetic.

The Ackermans' work was recognized early in their careers by inclusion in two influential exhibition series: *California Designed*, two shows organized by the Long Beach Municipal Art Center in conjunction with Bay Area venues in 1955 and 1956, and *California Design*, 21 shows organized mainly by the Pasadena Art Museum from 1954 to 1976. These exhibitions helped launch numerous artists and put California on the national map as a trendsetter in craft, design, and popular culture. "When *California Design* came along, it was a big boost for everybody in the design field—the craftsmen, artists, architects, even potential customers," Jerry explained. "The exposure cannot be overestimated. With each show, you could see the progression of new designs."

The first annual *California Design* exhibition was launched in winter 1954–1955 by the Pasadena Art Museum as a West Coast counterpart to New York's Museum of Modern Art's influential *Good Design* exhibitions. This was followed by annual exhibitions from 1956 to 1962, triennials in 1965, 1968, and 1971, and *California Design '76: A Bicentennial Celebration.* The first seven shows displayed a broad selection of home furnishings, decorative accessories, and household consumer goods. Clifford Nelson, then director of the museum, initiated the first five annuals, laying the foundation for what became the state's most renowned showcase of craft and design objects. Under the leadership of the arts visionary Eudorah M. Moore (1918–2013), beginning with the eighth *California Design* exhibition in 1962, a jury system was established. Later shows expanded in scope to include prototypes and one-of-a-kind experimental objects. These exhibitions and accompanying publications were testaments to Moore's belief that California was "an incubator for contemporary design." The *California Design* shows gained national publicity. In 1958 Arthur Millier, the art critic for the *Los Angeles Times*, declared, "Our artists are now taking their place in the world stream of art. . . . *California Design* has become a term touched with magic and spoken with respect."

The Ackermans had the rare distinction of being accepted into every *California Design* exhibition, with over 50 of their works spanning multiple categories, underscoring the couple's importance as mid-century California designer-craftsmen. The Ackermans exemplified Eudorah Moore's objective in presenting the *California Design* exhibitions, "to foster and promote the recognition of good design, and of designers of excellence."

OPPOSITE First shown in *California Designed* at the Long Beach Municipal Art Center and the San Francisco De Young Memorial Museum, Jenev ceramics appeared on the cover of the January 22, 1956, *Los Angeles Times Home* magazine.

OVERLEAF *Los Angeles Times* art critic Arthur Millier wrote about Southern California ceramicists who "are not overburdened by the weight of the past [but] create out of an incredibly flowering present." The 1958 gathering of the American Ceramic Society included the Ackermans, Peter Voulkos, Malcolm Leland, David Cressy, Raul Coronel, and Otto and Vivika Heino.

54
Bath and Wien

Some of the faces behind 'California Design'

THE Greater Los Angeles area, with smaller centers strung along the coast from Santa Barbara to San Diego, is now the scene of a regional surge of the arts of design. This movement shares in and is inspired by the phenomenal population growth which has compelled new solutions to many of the problems of community life. Like the new Southern California which has literally burst upon us in the past three decades, our art movement is young in spirit. From being a provincial affair only slightly in touch with artistic developments elsewhere in the world, it has become a movement of significance throughout the civilized world.

Our artists are now taking their place in the world stream of art. They are at home in the past and present arts of all nations and their works are seen throughout the world. California Design has become a term touched with magic and spoken with respect. Whether the product be a painting or a chair, a house or serigraph (silk-screen print), a sculptured piece, a textile or a mosaic, an artistic creation from Southern California, thanks to the adventuring spirit of this region, will generally be contemporary in style and young in spirit.

On the following pages Virginia Stewart introduces typical artists who work in this continually expanding field. She shows them and their creations in pictures and describes their activities and the uses to which their works are put. The section can offer only a sampling of a widespread activity, for the Los Angeles area is now next only to New York in the number of its residet artists. Miss Stewart, who died shortly after completing this assignment, was eminently qualified to present such a survey. For many years she explored among the artists, art craftsmen and designers of this region, coming to this field from a background of art-museum experience. Her articles appeared regularly in the Times Home Magazine.

The very remoteness of Los Angeles from other art centers has contributed to the youthful spirit inspiring our contemporary art. Our artists are aware of what is being done elsewhere, they visit the great art museums to the east and in Europe, but they are not overburdened by the weight of the past. They create out of an incredibly flowering present. They live and work at the center of a new way of living.

They live differently from artists in other world or national metropolises. Southern California's artists are not crowded into garrets or loft buildings. Their studios are surrounded by flowers and trees. They have homes and families. The outdoors is open to them. They do not think and work in packs or cults. They are strikingly individual in their attitudes toward life and in their ways of working. These things, the climate and the expanding character of the region have all contributed to the contemporary growth of the arts in Southern California. Art schools, colleges and universities are training art students to fill the needs of a public growing in numbers and sophistication. Los Angeles may yet become the art center of the nation.

by ARTHUR MILLIER
Times Art Critic

tographed at *a recent Los Angeles exhibit are, at left, members of design division, Southern California section, American Ceramic ety. Standing, back row, from left: Peter Voulkos, Raul onel, Louisa and Albert King, Malcolm Leland, Jerome and Evelyn erman, David Cressy; middle row: Sue Shrode, Bernard Kester, ka Heino; lower row: John Harding, Otto Heino, John Mason Susan Peterson. All are well known in local art circles*

ACKERMAN WORKS IN CALIFORNIA DESIGNED AND CALIFORNIA DESIGN

***CALIFORNIA DESIGNED* 1955**
LONG BEACH MUNICIPAL ART CENTER /
M. H. DE YOUNG MEMORIAL MUSEUM
Covered jar, black and white
Bottle with stopper, black and white
Bowl, black and white
Covered jar, white and stars
Vase, white and stars
Cigarette cup, white and stars
Plate, decorated blue and white
Decanter, decorated
Bird bowl, white with blue center
Tray, black

***CALIFORNIA DESIGNED* 1956**
LONG BEACH MUNICPAL ART CENTER /
OAKLAND ART MUSEUM
Walnut coffee table with mosaic top
Two Girls in the Rain [Two Women Under Umbrella], mosaic panel
Houses at Night [Byzantia], mosaic panel
Warrior King, cast aluminum plaque

CALIFORNIA DESIGN I
PASADENA ART MUSEUM, 1954–1955
Cigarette cups (2)
Bowls (2)
Bottle with stopper
Oval plates (2)

CALIFORNIA DESIGN II
PASADENA ART MUSEUM, 1956
Three Musicians, bas-relief plaque
Lonely Boy, sculpture

CALIFORNIA DESIGN III
PASADENA ART MUSEUM, 1957
Hot Bird, tapestry
Warrior King, cast aluminum plaque
Mermaid, mosaic panel

CALIFORNIA DESIGN IV
PASADENA ART MUSEUM, 1958
Kites, silk screen hanging
Partridge, mosaic panel
Elipses, mosaic panel
Falconer [Knight on Horse], tapestry
Byzantia Night, mosaic panel

CALIFORNIA DESIGN V
PASADENA ART MUSEUM, 1959
Birds in Tree, tapestry
Pennants, mosaic panel
Girl with Flowers, tapestry
Saint George and the Dragon, carved wood panel
Adhara Abstract, mosaic panel

CALIFORNIA DESIGN VI
PASADENA ART MUSEUM, 1960
King, tapestry
Queen, tapestry
Equestrian, rug
Venetian Dusk, rug
Sunburst, rug
Diamonds, rug

CALIFORNIA DESIGN VII
PASADENA ART MUSEUM, 1961
Garden of Eden (triptych), carved wood
Birds of a Feather, tapestry
Hot Summer Landscape, tapestry
Flower Abstract, tapestry

CALIFORNIA DESIGN VIII
PASADENA ART MUSEUM, 1962
Mother and Child, tapestry
Canal, tapestry, cool colors
Canal, tapestry, warm colors
Tapestry Abstract, tapestry
Monkeys, hooked wall hanging
King and Queen, door pulls
Lapis Horse, door pull
Turquoise Horse, door pull
Abstract, mosaic panel

CALIFORNIA DESIGN IX
PASADENA ART MUSEUM, 1965
Antico hardware
Finger puppets
Buildings, tapestry
Cat and Bird, tapestry
Warriors, carved wood panel
Arbole, tapestry
Wedding, hooked wall hanging
Cloth Doll

CALIFORNIA DESIGN X
PASADENA ART MUSEUM /
CALIFORNIA EXPOSITION, 1968
Op 66, tapestry

CALIFORNIA DESIGN XI
PASADENA ART MUSEUM, 1971
Launch Pad, tapestry
Animals, carved wood blocks
Campesina, tapestry
Labyrinth, tapestry
Aerial View, tapestry
Blocks, tapestry

CALIFORNIA DESIGN '76: A BICENTENNIAL CELEBRATION
PACIFIC DESIGN CENTER, 1976
California Poppies, embroidered hanging

OPPOSITE The October 1966 issue of *House & Garden* magazine featured finger puppets that Evelyn originally designed as a fundraiser for the La Playa Co-op Nursery School that their daughter, Laura, attended. Kits for the puppets included all the materials needed, instructions, and a photograph of the finished piece. Eventually sold through ERA, the puppets were selected for *California Design IX*. ABOVE RIGHT *California Design* provided hangtags and labels for marketing.

A MARRIAGE OF ART AND COMMERCE

DAVID A. KEEPS

Imagine a time and a place before computers and smart phones—let's call it Detroit, in the autumn of 1948—when meeting the girl of your dreams took confidence and initiative. On the advice of a friend, a charismatic 28-year-old World War II vet named Jerome Ackerman, armed with charm and two candy bars in his pocket, pays a visit to the Lucé Lipton Interior Design Studio. There, he spies Lucé's 24-year-old sister-in-law, Evelyn, busily folding fabric samples. She is the most dazzling woman Jerome has ever seen. His heart jumps to his throat, but his voice—a lyric baritone so rich and true he might have been a big band singer—does not falter.

"I said, 'Hi, I'm Jerry Ackerman,'" he recalled, when telling the story, admitting he was trying to be suave. "'Would you like a Milky Way?' And fortunately, she liked chocolate."

More than the candy, the lovely and talented but shy Evelyn also liked Jerry's easy, sociable manner. Though they had grown up in the same neighborhood, they had met only once, briefly, at Wayne University in Detroit, where they had both studied art. And on this chilly day, there were fireworks. "I just knew he knew he was right for me," Evelyn said delightedly whenever Jerry retold the tale. "I would've married him that very day." She was so smitten that she even gave up a ticket to Paris where she had planned to continue studying art.

So began a love affair that spanned seven decades and a working relationship that produced an unrivaled range of mid-20th century artistry and craft. Opposites yet soulmates, Jerry and Evelyn became husband and wife in September, 1948, and together formed a strong and equal union that defined their personal lives and their professional pursuits, and married art and commerce. Raised during the Great Depression of the 1930s, they had learned frugality, self-sufficiency, and the value of education. Continuing their studies at Wayne University, they lived on GI Bill supplements and made their own furniture and decorations for their first apartment. As newlyweds, they attended the Detroit Institute of Arts' *For Modern Living*, an exhibition mounted by the architect Alexander Girard. The eye-opening show featured the groundbreaking work of another young couple, Charles and Ray Eames, who had met at the Cranbrook Academy of Art in suburban Detroit.

"We thought, if they could do it, why can't we?" Jerry often remarked. "At least we could try." Though they were studying fine art and Jerry was also pursuing an art teaching credential, the Ackermans immersed themselves in crafts. They were highly influenced by the intersection of art, design, and mass production espoused by the Bauhaus movement that had helped shape modern architecture and home design. Despite their limited resources, the Ackermans embraced the romance of adventure and opportunity, meeting artists, architects, and designers, and traveling when and where they could—in a Raymond Loewy–designed Studebaker—before making Los Angeles their home in 1952.

In Southern California, where, Jerry said, "we weren't freezing our asses off," their talents blossomed. With intellectual rigor, physical dexterity, an eye for beauty, and an inventive approach to their work, Jerry and Evelyn mastered ceramics, mosaics, textiles, woodcarving, and metalwork. They created beautiful and affordable decorative objects that brought much-needed hand-wrought warmth and texture into small-scale postwar modern homes. Gifted at both colorful abstraction and a distinctively sweet storybook figurative style that embraced folk and modern art as well as 1950s and 1960s commercial illustration, the Ackermans produced designs that transferred effortlessly to whatever media and materials they tackled. Channeling California's sunny spirit, Evelyn's optimistic, often whimsical renderings of flowers, animals, children, and mythical figures delighted mid-century homeowners. Her designs became part of an international decorative arts canon that includes the work of Alexander Girard, Bjørn Wiinblad, Stig Lindberg, Sascha Brastoff, and Georges Briard.

The endurance of the Ackermans' work is a testament to their skills not only as designer-craftspersons, but also as creators of an independent, owner-operated business. In a world that predated e-commerce, eBay, and Etsy, Jerry built their brand with shoe-leather perseverance. A natural salesman who had hawked newspapers as a boy, Jerry traveled to trade shows, furniture markets, and contemporary home-decor stores with his first 1953–1954 collection of ceramics, which bore the name Jenev (a contraction of "Jerry" and "Evelyn" that, Jerry liked to say "sounded European"). The celebrated New York modernist designer Paul McCobb purchased pieces for his home—which at the time sold for $1 to $17 and now fetch considerably more—and also showcased the line in his Directional Furniture showrooms.

In 1956 when the Ackermans launched ERA Industrias (with their Detroit friend, the architect Sherrill Broudy) and expanded their offerings to include new designs, they searched the world to source skilled artisans to execute accessibly priced, limited runs of mosaics and textiles. They sold these items at wholesale prices to interior decorators and architects at a Los Angeles to-the-trade showroom they opened in the early 1960s. Often featured on the cover of the *Los Angeles Times Home* magazine and in exhibitions—including every one of the prestigious *California*

OPPOSITE Ka Kwong Hui, a friend of the Ackermans at Alfred University, recommended a patternmaker in Hornell, New York, to handmake Jerry's kick wheel. In the Jenev studio, Jerry examined a plate he had just thrown for Evelyn to decorate. At far left, is Jerry's first pot from Wayne University and at far right, a pot made at Alfred. OVERLEAF At Wayne, Jerry enrolled in David Mitchell's painting class in 1950, producing *Triangles in Flight* for an assignment.

Design shows from 1954 to 1976—the Ackermans' designs were purchased not only for individual residences, but also for hotels, restaurants, public buildings, and corporate offices.

"In older civilizations, handcrafts were generally unique creations commissioned by a patron; the tapestries and ceramic designs of the palazzi of the Medici, for example, were to be seen nowhere else," the Ackermans astutely told Billie Kolb Youngblood in a 1963 *Interior Previews West Coast Sourcebook*. "Our investment of time and overhead in a design cannot be recouped in a single piece. But it is possible, without running the risk of having a design seen so often as to be trite, to spread costs and bring original creations to the American scene."

In practice, they did more than just manage the economics of handcrafted works. Updating ancient mosaic and weaving techniques with a playful 1950s exuberance, their designs revitalized those crafts and came to define the California modernist movement and its place in decor during the postwar housing boom. One of their wall hangings, *Garden*, was so iconic that it was depicted in a 1963 men's magazine cartoon set in a modernist living room. "You really know you've made it when you see your work in *Playboy*," Jerry joked.

And the Ackermans' work continues to inspire contemporary artisans, from small-batch craftsmen to mass-market design retailers, including Jonathan Adler. Ackerman designs have soared in value, said Peter Loughrey, the founder of Los Angeles Modern Auctions. "They were incredibly prolific, and really understood what people wanted," he noted. "They produced the same designs in both cool blues and greens, and in warm tones of red and yellow, to coordinate with the color schemes of their customers' homes."

Their business also evolved to serve the architecture and design market, adding carved wood panels and cabinetry hardware to their own line and representing international craft-based products in their showroom.

My first impression of the Ackermans was indelible—two people so utterly in love and in sync with one another and their work that they seemed to function as one. In 2006 as a reporter for the *Los Angeles Times* Home section, I was invited to the 20th century California design gallery Reform to see a collection of their work. "They're amazing," said Gerard O'Brien, the owner, who had sought out the Ackermans to authenticate pieces and subsequently became friends with them. "You're going to love them."

Neither he nor I had any idea just how much I would love them. In the loft on the second floor, which O'Brien had artfully arranged with tapestries, woodcarvings, and mosaics, Jerry had spread out press clippings, catalogs, and brochures. One of them bore the logo of J. L. Hudson, the Detroit department store that anchored the 1954 Victor Gruen–designed Northland Center, where I had roamed as a suburban youth.

"Oh," I said, "You sold your work at my department store?"

"I didn't know you owned it," wisecracked Jerry, then 86, but still wielding the same humor he had employed the first time he met his future wife. "Are you from Detroit? We are."

I one-upped him, guessing he had probably attended my parents' alma mater, Central High. Indeed, he had. I fished my phone out of my pocket and called home. "Dad," I asked, "Do you remember Jerry Ackerman?" "Well, son of a bitch!" my father replied. "He was class president."

"Hand it over," Jerry said, reaching for the phone. From that moment on, formality gave way to familiarity. I would often see Jerry and Evelyn at art and design events around Los Angeles—indeed, though it was my beat as a reporter, I usually first found out about them from Jerry—and he would inevitably greet me with two words: "Hey, kiddo!"

On my parents' next trip to Los Angeles, they went with me to the Ackerman home, a tract house in Culver City that they had purchased in 1956 from Evelyn's brother. Filled with classic mid-century furniture, folk art, their own early artworks from the 1940s, and their designs from the 1950s to the 1970s, it was a home that lived and breathed with a very personal history and yet felt timelessly modern. One of the kitchen walls was covered in carved wood *Zodiac* panels, and the cabinets had their exquisite *Antico* drawer pulls that had been hand cast in brass by Italian craftsmen. The living room had early Eames plywood chairs, Alvar Aalto stools, a Hans Wegner sewing table and chairs, and Evelyn's abstract mosaic table, *Cats*.

The adjoining studio, where Evelyn had produced hundreds of drawings and design prototypes, was now filled with the exquisite stoneware pottery Jerry had created as a graduate student in the 1950s and newer works he had produced since semiretiring in the 1990s. The space also housed some of Evelyn's collection of antique dolls and dollhouses, a passion that led her to develop doll-costume patterns and write five acclaimed scholarly books. On one wall were some of Evelyn's early cloisonnés, an intricate, enameled-metal artform she took up in her late 50s. Fearlessly diving into this medium, the thrill of this highly detailed craft prompted her to produce a series, *Stories from the Bible*, that now reside in the Renwick Gallery at the Smithsonian American Art Museum in Washington, D.C. "The cloisonnés were a work of passion. I was almost compelled to do them," she said of the miniature enamels. "It presented me with an intellectual and creative challenge to design a cohesive series of works that could illustrate a story within very small confines."

After touring their home, we enjoyed lunch that afternoon at their local deli, the Roll 'n Rye, and, on another visit the adventurous Ackermans introduced my folks to sushi at a restaurant near their Culver City home. Filled with recollections of their former high school classmates and long-gone but fondly remembered Detroit landmarks, these reunions made me appreciate the Ackermans for being risk-taking artists who had blazed their own trail without losing sight of their roots. In 2008 my parents and I joined

OPPOSITE In 1949 Evelyn posed with her still life in the couple's first apartment in Detroit. To save money, they made most of their furnishings. Evelyn sewed the draperies that were silk screened with Jerry's design by Ruben Eshkanian, who would later work for the textile designer Jack Lenor Larsen.

Jerry and Evelyn at the one-time home of Hollywood legend Gary Cooper designed by the architect A. Quincy Jones, where the Museum of California Design recognized the Ackermans' lifelong achievements. "Jerome and Evelyn embodied the can-do spirit of California, functioning as craftspeople, commercial designers, and producers," said the founder Bill Stern, upon presenting them with the organization's Henry Award. "Their work brought affordable mid-century design into homes across the country." There was a fundraising auction afterward, and I bought my parents a painting; they in turn surprised me by purchasing a wooden bas-relief depicting two birds that the Ackermans had designed for Panelcarve and donated to the sale. "I framed that yesterday, myself," Jerry told me, showing off his handiwork. "Well, of course you did," I replied, adding that the two carved lovebirds would henceforth be known as Evelyn and Jerry.

As a new breed of design fans, enamored of *Mad Men* and all things mid-century modern, began to discover and validate their work, it became clear that the Ackermans' star had risen again to illuminate the 21st century. In 2009, on the eve of a major retrospective of some 200 pieces at the Mingei International Museum in San Diego, I returned to their home to profile the Ackermans for the *Los Angeles Times*' "Masters of Craft" series. Jerry had a seemingly inexhaustible supply of stories: Evelyn's brief period of employment answering fan mail and correcting scripts for the comedian Red Skelton, a notorious ad libber, for a dollar an hour during their early years in Los Angeles and weekend poolside visits with Red and his wife Georgia at their home in Bel Air; their encounters with ceramic artists such as Gertrud and Otto Natzler, Peter Voulkos, and Harrison McIntosh, studio woodworker Sam Maloof, Architectural Pottery owners Max and Rita Lawrence, and Mexican designer José Pepe Mendoza. A walking Rolodex of mid-century modernism, Jerry talked about forging relationships with the most prominent and influential architects and architectural firms of the time, from Victor Gruen to Welton Becket, as well as pioneers of California mid-century architecture including Killingsworth, Brady & Smith and Donald Wexler. He recounted conversations with real estate developer Joseph Eichler, working on commercial and residential projects with interior designers like Arthur Elrod, and sales calls to large department stores throughout the country.

Dressed in a white shirt, with a black sweater and slacks and an impeccable biomorphic design she had cut from sheet silver for a necklace some 60 years earlier, Evelyn sat quietly, beaming at her beloved husband. And with the energy of a man half his age, Jerry unearthed kits they had designed for making finger puppets, unfurled sketches for tapestries, complete with yarn samples, and unrolled a magnificent 6-by-8-foot tapestry commissioned for the Beverly Hills office of the Litton Corporation.

Looking through it all, the breadth of their work was impressive, from the primary-colored Calder-esque minimalism of a woven wool tapestry called *Striped Candy Tree* to the delicacy and moodiness of *Rain*, a mosaic showing two figures under umbrellas scurrying through the bluster of a storm. "I would go to the showroom and come back to find Evy with a stack of drawings," he said about their early days. "She'd say, 'These are for wood, those are for weavings, and the others are for mosaics.' It astonished me that this fine artist who had never done anything commercial could come up with these things."

Looking back, Jerry confessed, "We never thought about being part of this time period that would be designated as important. It reaffirms the faith that you had in what you were doing, and that you struck a responsive chord." Evelyn added her own perspective. "One of our goals was to be affordable—not having a lot of money was the position we were in most of our young life, so that is what we strove to do for others," she declared for that *Los Angeles Times* feature. "The work was meant to be appealing, but it was never frivolous."

"I often wondered how I came to find and marry this remarkable woman," Jerry has said of his wife. "Evy simply said it was meant to be." She, in turn, called Jerry her Svengali. "How many couples can work together and last? Not many. If I couldn't do something, Jerry did it. If he couldn't do it, I did. We just worked all the time; it's what we wanted to do. We were a perfect match."

Over the course of their remarkable lives and career, Jerry and Evelyn produced not only enduring and endearing works of art, but also crafted relationships that continue to flourish. Both agreed that as artists and people, their greatest creation was their daughter, Laura, who inspired so much of their joyful work and who, since Evelyn's passing in November 2012, and Jerry's in March 2019, carries the Ackerman legacy forward with Ackerman Modern. Theirs is a romantic story worth honoring and passing down, a primer for a successful artistic marriage. Possessed of a singular vision, the talented couple made the world a lovelier place, with heartfelt, sophisticated designs that will touch lives for generations. In this book, it is a distinct honor to introduce Jerome and Evelyn Ackerman and the work and the life they made together.

OPPOSITE Looking through an opening in the largest of the kilns at Alfred University in Upstate New York, Jerry checked on the cones that indicated the temperature. The cones bent as the temperature increased, and once it reached cone level 10—required for stoneware—the kiln was shut off. OVERLEAF Evelyn typed the 1957 Era Industrias price list.

Part II
Building a Business

ERA I

2207 Federal Avenue . Los Angele

PRICE LIST

Pr[illegible]es Subject To Change Without Notice.

ITEM

NO. SIZE TITLE

VENETIAN GLASS MOSAIC PANELS - wal

Artists: Jerome and Evelyn Ackerman, Sh

101....12"x36"...PARTRIDGE. Figure:
beige-yellow. Bkgd.

201....12"x36"...HOT BIRD. Figure: or
turq.-black. Bkgd.:

202....12"x36"...BIRD. Figure: orange-
black. Bkgd.: brown

301....12"x60"...MERMAID. Figure: wh
Bkgd.: blue-greens.

302....12"x48"...LION. (Figures: tans-

303....12"x48"...TIGER. (Bkgd.: white;

501....20"x48"...WOMEN UNDER UMBR
white-pink. Bkgd.:

502A...16"x36"...BIRDS IN SUN. Figure
orange-red. Bkgd.:

504....16"x36"...WARRIOR. Figure: tan
Bkgd.: browns-gold-

505A...16"x35"...CAT & FLOWERS. Fig

STRIAS
4, California . Granite 8-1995

January 1957

	RETAIL PRICE
finish wood frames.	
ll Broudy.	
k-purple-turq.-	$ 67.50
hite.	
e-pink-ochre-	67.50
ite.	
-yellow-turq.-	67.50
o whites.	
-gray-pinks.	110.00
low-rust-orange.)............	87.50
ves: blue-greens.)............	87.50
A. Figures:	225.00
-black-purple.	
llows-pink-	100.00
-turq.	
hre-blue-white.	90.00
ck.	
: blue-black on	90.00

JENEV DESIGN STUDIO

JO LAURIA AND DALE CAROLYN GLUCKMAN

In December 1952, soon after the Ackermans moved to California, they rented a 1,000-square-foot industrial space in West Los Angeles for $66 a month and launched their first business—Jenev Design Studio. The couple thought it imparted a sophisticated flair. Short on cash but long on talent, ingenuity, and youthful optimism, the young designer-craftsmen put into practice their belief that those qualities, along with enthusiasm and hard work, would enable them to succeed. The Ackermans outfitted their studio on a limited budget with the necessary equipment, including a large used Denver kiln for $200. Evelyn's meticulous budgeting accounted for purchases of clay and glaze materials, tools, and basic supplies essential to an operating studio. To supplement their income while developing Jenev, the couple also designed decorative kitchen and bath items for Cal Pacific, a friend's ceramic import business. At the same time, Evelyn worked for the comedian Red Skelton to help make ends meet.

The couple soon realized they could not financially survive by creating and selling one-of-a-kind wheel-thrown ceramics and understood why many of their "pottery friends" held teaching positions to augment their incomes. Instead, they brought their creativity and commitment to quality, limited-production slip-cast ceramics. Jerry's extensive technical training as a graduate student in ceramics at Alfred University provided the necessary background to establish a ceramic studio and motivated him to explore the slip-casting technique, knowing this industrial method was an efficient means of producing multiples. The Ackermans viewed this approach as the quickest way to launch their business. Some pieces were glazed in minimalist matte-finish black and/or white "because it was simple and clean and would go with anything," as Jerry was fond of remarking. Others were blue and white or embellished with incised or stylized majolica stars or striped patterns in blue, green, or rust. Evelyn decorated select pieces using the specialized techniques of sgraffito or Mishima.

The Ackermans received national recognition for their Jenev ceramics as they were featured in *House Beautiful*. They continued to participate in national ceramic shows during this time, and Jenev's pieces were featured in exhibitions, including *Young Americans* and the *Los Angeles County Fair Arts of Daily Living* in 1954 and *California Designed* and *California Design I* in 1955. On April 12, 1955, the *Detroit News* ran a story "Artists Pool Names, Talents in California Pottery Venture." The writer, Joy Hakanson, noted that "By combining their names and their talents, two former Detroiters created a new trademark in ceramics. . . . Their California studio is less than three years old. Yet it has made a strong bid for national attention." The Jenev ceramic product line now consisted of 46 offerings ranging from cups to vases to bowls. The Jenev studio had become a viable and successful endeavor as a result of the talent and hard work of its founders.

In 1955 an exhibition of mosaics the couple saw in San Francisco inspired Evelyn to experiment with that technique. Initially the Ackermans focused on making mosaic-topped coffee tables and did both the design and execution. Jerry developed the table shapes and sourced Los Angeles-based suppliers to create rectangular, square, and round frames in wood or metal.

The Jenev years were marked by experimentation with varied materials and diverse techniques. In yet another outlet for Evelyn's creativity, she developed designs on linen, felt, and window-shade material, which were hand-printed by a professional silk screener in Los Angeles. Like the mosaics, these were well-suited to residential applications. Intent on broadening their distinctive product line, Jerry also executed their designs in sand-cast aluminum and cast cement.

Further, Jerry took on the responsibility for directly marketing their products. His first sale was to Jules Seltzer, the owner of a prominent modernist furniture showroom in Los Angeles. Jerry later recalled that selling the ceramics "so intimately associated with my ego, my skills" made him nervous. "The first day I went out to make a call, I made a sale to Jules Seltzer for $40, then I went to Leslie's and made another sale for $100. I was thrilled at the response." With his ready wit and outgoing personality, Jerry marketed Jenev products to well-known retailers such as W. & J. Sloane, Barker Brothers, and J. L. Hudson, as well as to prestigious showrooms like Carroll Sagar and Associates and Paul McCobb. Initially, McCobb and his wife collected Jenev ceramics for their own home. McCobb later decided to distribute Jenev ceramics through his Directional Furniture showrooms in Los Angeles and New York, and at the Chicago Merchandise Mart, beginning in 1954 and included them in advertising and publicity. The Ackermans immediately realized that this represented "a very big step as it helped introduce us to the national marketplace."

OPPOSITE The group of ceramics displayed against colorful backdrops in the Jenev studio highlighted a variety of shapes, glazes, and decoration techniques. The Eames chair, bought from Herman Miller in Michigan, was packed in their Plymouth station wagon for the move to California. OVERLEAF The second Jenev brochure, designed by Burt Anderson, a friend who was an artist for Hughes Aircraft, showed functional yet decorative objects. PAGES 56–57 The Ackermans introduced a line of mosaic tables in the mid-1950s. Model 301-W, which retailed for $275, had a round abstract mosaic top set in a 36-inch solid walnut frame with a hand-rubbed oil finish that subtly echoed the shape of the inset. Due to the size of the tables, sales representatives were given sample boards with photographs. This best-seller was exhibited in *California Designed* 1955.

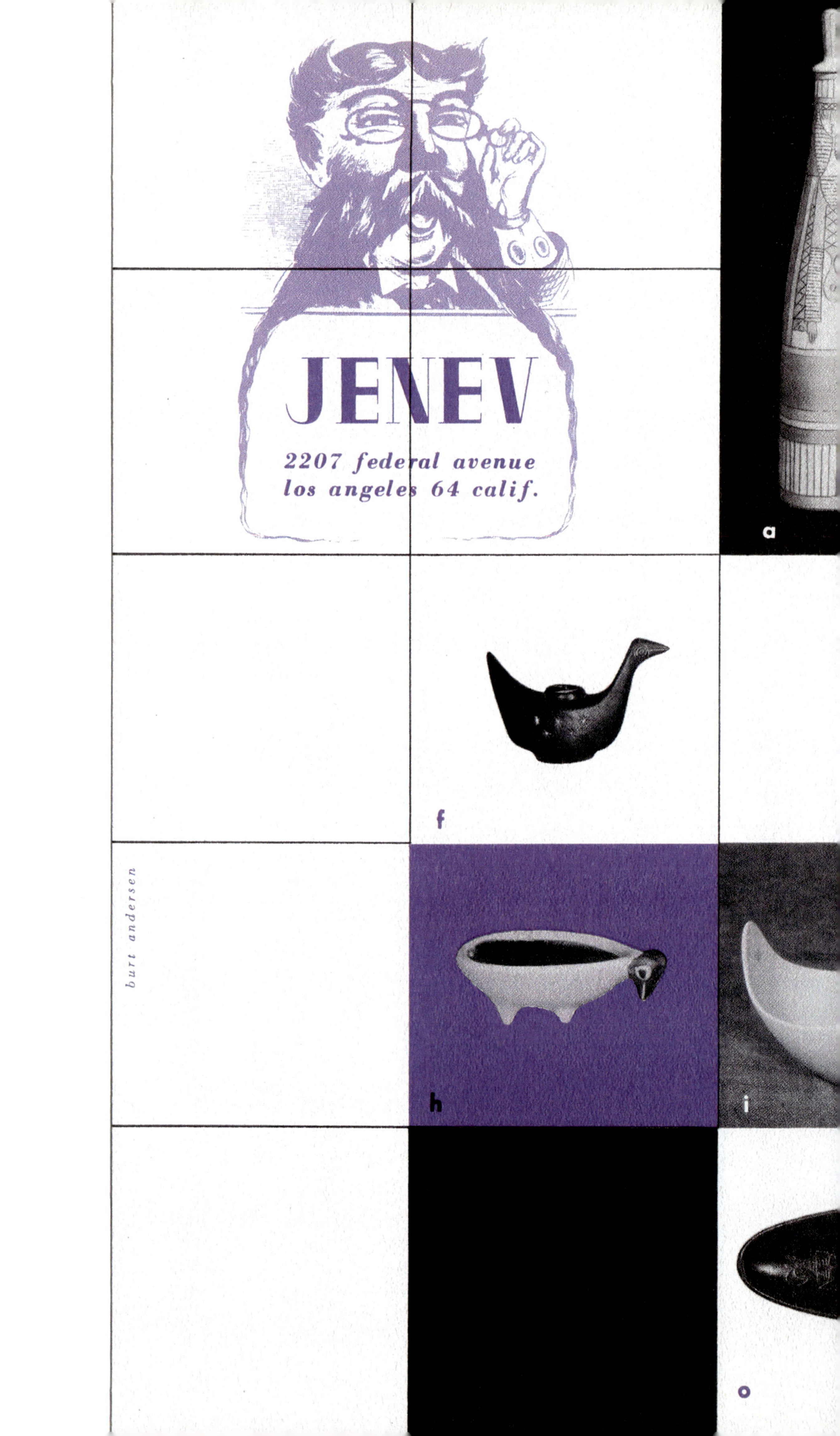
JENEV
2207 federal avenue
los angeles 64 calif.
a
f
burt andersen
h
i
o

b
c
d
e
g
j
k
l
m
n

JENEV

301 - W

ERA INDUSTRIES

DALE CAROLYN GLUCKMAN AND JO LAURIA

The story of ERA Industries begins in 1956 when Jerry reconnected with Sherrill Broudy, an old school friend from Detroit who was working with the architect Victor Gruen. A commercial partnership was formed, and Jenev evolved into ERA Industrias, charting the beginning of a new business venture focused on delivering designs to the burgeoning post-World War II home furnishings market.

The partnership, though short-lived, encouraged the Ackermans to expand their repertoire of designs. While many designer-craftsmen were known for working in one medium and style, the Ackermans' creative expression was multifaceted. Utilizing an innovative combination of traditional techniques and modern production methods, the Ackermans became known for their diversity—designing decorative accessories and architectural elements in textiles, wood, mosaic, metal, and Hydrastone that were distributed nationally. Throughout their careers, the entrepreneurial Ackermans stayed true to themselves as artists "driven by what we wanted to do as artist craftsmen, what we thought was missing from the market for consumers."

By 1963, now known as ERA Industries, the company had already made its mark with a diverse catalog of more than 200 products. At the heart of this success were Jerry and Evelyn Ackerman whose complementary talents formed the company's backbone. Evelyn took on the role of primary designer, her creative vision spanning an impressive range of styles from geometric minimalism to biomorphic abstraction to whimsical stylization. She had a sophisticated eye for line, color, and form and the rare ability to design across a wide range of materials to create works vastly different in scale, from small woven hangings to large architectural mosaics. Many of their colorful textiles and mosaics were made in cool and warm colorways to work with different interior palettes. Jerry, with his keen business acumen, managed production, sales, and marketing, ensuring they reached a broad market. As demand grew, they realized the need to expand beyond self-production. The Ackermans adapted new methods of production that combined handwork with semi-industrial processes. Additionally, they established relationships with skilled artisans in other countries, allowing for limited production runs that maintained quality while keeping prices affordable. Their products were "governed by a simple principle of supply and demand." If sales of a design dwindled, it was discontinued when the inventory ran out.

ERA's product lines soon expanded beyond the Ackermans' own designs. In their catalogs and showroom, they featured the work of select craftspeople who met their exacting standards, importing handcrafted items from across the globe including Pepe Mendoza accessories, Don Shoemaker furniture, South American crafts, contemporary European and Scandinavian products, and Aubusson tapestries. This diverse portfolio allowed ERA products to appeal to the tastes of a broad clientele and fit into a wide range of stylistic interiors.

ERA's products found their way into major department stores like J. L. Hudson, Macy's, and Neiman Marcus, while also being distributed through wholesale channels to contract furnishings, interior design, and architectural markets. Their relationships with important architects—Gensler, Victor Gruen, Skidmore, Owings & Merrill, Pereira & Luckman, Welton Becket, Richard Dorman, Kanner & Mayer, Palmer & Krisel, Craig Ellwood, and A. Quincy Jones—could not be underestimated. The interior designers Arthur Elrod, Howard Hirsch, Henry End, Steve Chase, Harold Grieve, Cannell & Chaffin, and Saphier, Lerner, Schindler were frequent customers. The Ackermans sold to contemporary stores Carroll Sagar and Associates, Frasers, Van Keppel-Green, Curt Wagner, Frank Brothers, and Siebert's. Magazine photographers and set designers frequently borrowed pieces.

The Ackermans created the content and layout for ads and marketing materials themselves. Jerry, while continuing to make calls personally, developed a network of sales representatives across the country. In Detroit it was Ruth Adler Schnee's father, Joseph Schnee. By the late 1950s, they began exhibiting at major trade shows, constantly introducing new designs to meet market demand. Jerry ensured coverage in trade magazines including *Contract*, *Interiors*, and *Sourcebook*, but perhaps the most important "publicity you couldn't buy" came from the *Los Angeles Times Home* magazine, which frequently featured ERA products in their articles.

ERA's reputation for high-quality and original products led to numerous special commissions. Perhaps their most ambitious project was a series of a dozen 6-by-8-foot needlepoint wall hangings created for Litton Industries' corporate offices in Beverly Hills. This two-year project, beginnning in 1968 and made in Greece, showcased Evelyn's artistic prowess and ERA's ability to coordinate complex, large-scale works.

As their business grew, so did their physical presence in the design world. In 1959 they opened their first showroom on Melrose Avenue in Los Angeles. By 1964, they had moved to a larger space on Beverly Boulevard, on the same block as Herman Miller and Jules Seltzer, positioning themselves at the heart of the city's design community. Their final move in 1979 to the Pacific Design Center with Forms+Surfaces solidified their status as a design force.

The era of ERA came to a close in the early 1980s, but its impact on the design world endures. The Ackermans' collaborative venture left a legacy of distinctly modernist artistic sensibility. Their story is not just one of business success but a lifelong dedication to well-crafted design.

OPPOSITE Jerry sits in a leather and rosewood chair by Don Shoemaker, a Mexico-based American designer they represented. Evelyn stands by handwoven tapestries displayed on wings used to maximize the wall space in the ERA showroom.

ABOVE When the Ackermans moved their showroom to Beverly Boulevard in the heart of the Los Angeles design trade in 1964, Evelyn combined the ERA signage letters with free-form embellishments. Murray Feldman, a friend who was later the vice president of the Pacific Design Center, rented the Ackermans a space adjacent to his Chairs Unlimited showroom and opposite the Eames-designed Herman Miller showroom. OPPOSITE The first ERA showroom at 8703 Melrose Avenue, Los Angeles, displayed Ackerman products alongside hardware and tables by Pepe Mendoza. To better serve their to-the-trade clients, the Ackermans showcased the work of selected craftsmen from Finnish Takanas to Zapotec rugs to American ceramic sculptures. OVERLEAF The first ERA catalog, featuring many of the mosaics, offered "the finest expression of contemporary design, each executed with custom craftsmanship." This commitment to design and craft was a hallmark of Ackerman products for all the years they were in business.

ERA
designs by EVELYN ACKERMAN
8103

ERA INDUSTRIAS presents an exciting collection of colorful venetian glass mosaic pictures, handu
sculptured plaques by distinguished American artists. These wall hangings are the finest express
design, each executed with custom craftsmanship. They enhance an interior with dramatic distinc
506
302
303
502A
* MURAL
301
ERA

es, and

nporary

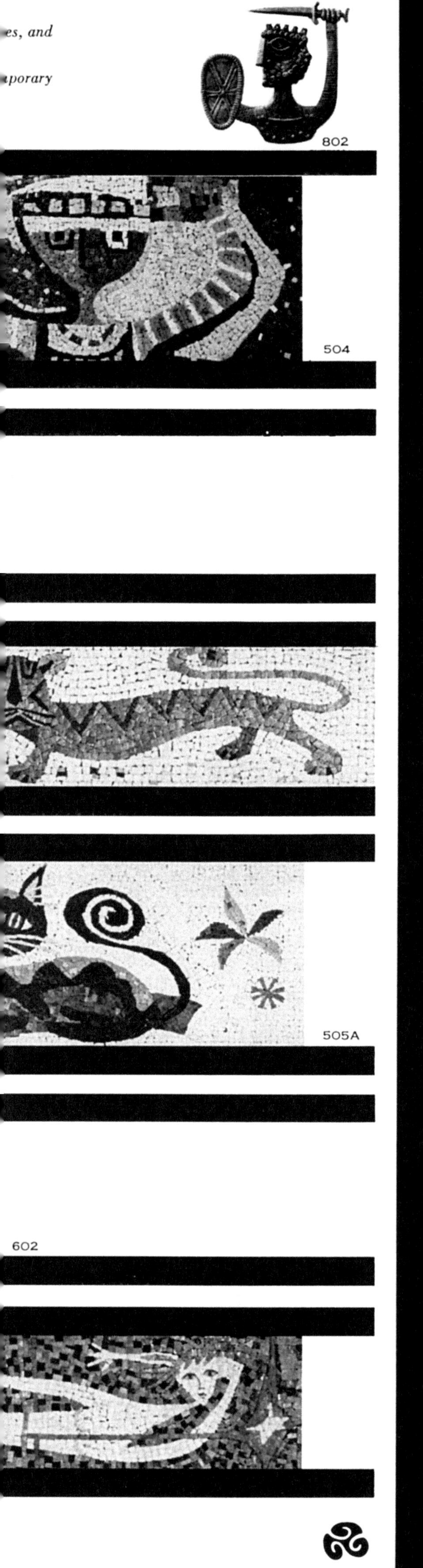

802

504

505A

602

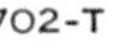

202

601

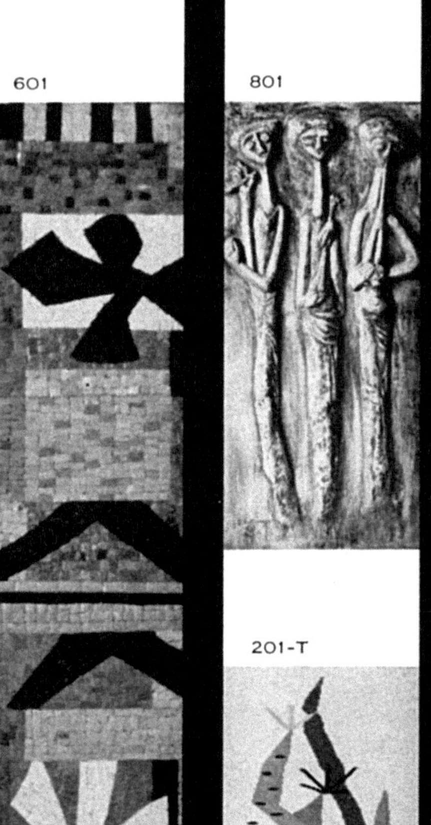

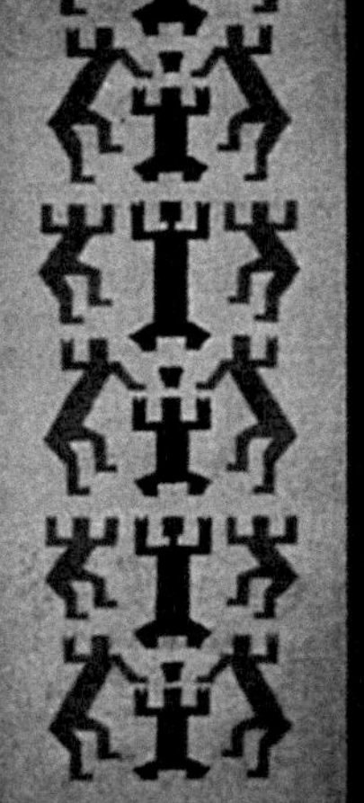

702-T

801

201-T

201

101

501

ERA INDUSTRIAS · 2207 FEDERAL AVENUE · LOS ANGELES 4, CALIFORNIA

Part III
Exploring Materials

fringe
DARK ORANGE

MATERIAL CURIOSITY BY DESIGN

DANIELLE CHARLAP

Long before Evelyn and Jerome Ackerman started their successful interior decor business, they were art students learning a multitude of techniques. The young designers experimented with painting, sculpture, ceramics, weaving, metalwork, and silk screening, continuously propelled to explore new mediums and skills. Although their first company, Jenev, initially only sold Jerome's slip-cast ceramics, this singular focus was the anomaly of their career. Their company soon became synonymous with a colorful medley of designs produced in a wide array of materials.

Throughout their practice, the Ackermans retained a sensitivity to process and materiality. As Evelyn explained in 1963, "Before you can design successfully, it is necessary not only to visualize the possibilities of the medium, but also to understand and respect the limits of the technique." In the mid-1950s Evelyn and Jerry did just that, seeking instruction from an Alfred University friend on how to assemble mosaics. They became intimately familiar with the process, creating mosaic tabletops, wall panels, and public commissions by hand before eventually turning to other craftspeople to produce Evelyn's designs. After they founded ERA Industrias (later ERA Industries) in 1956, the Ackermans increasingly hired craftspeople around the world to fabricate their products. For some techniques such as weaving, hooking, needlepoint, woodcarving, silk screen, and metal casting, they were indebted to artisans in Mexico, Japan, Italy, Greece, and the United States, whose talents allowed the Ackermans to push their material exploration beyond their own training. Sending samples, detailed drawings, and correspondence back and forth, the Ackermans worked closely with other makers to bring their designs to life in an ever-expanding variety of media.

*Flower Garden (*originally titled *Flower Abstract* when shown in *California Design VII)* epitomizes the Ackermans' interest in material reinterpretation. With its vivid colors emphasized through Evelyn's play with contrast, *Flower Garden* reflects the Ackermans' flair for simplified, abstracted mid-century design. Evelyn appreciated how expressing the same design in different materials could create equally striking yet distinct effects. Produced as a mosaic and a weaving by craftspeople in Mexico, *Flower Garden* received attention for both forms. On June 28, 1959, the *Los Angeles Times Home* magazine printed a photograph of the mosaic and textile together. Beyond making clear the difference in scale, the image underscored their individual textural qualities—the undulating color variation of the mosaic's small, tiled pieces a clear departure from the saturated color fields of the weaving. As the caption pointed out, the photograph immediately "illustrat[es] graphically the differing nature and characteristics of these two popular art forms." In 1961, while the seventh annual *California Design* exhibition included only the *Flower Garden* tapestry, *Arts & Architecture* magazine still showed both versions in its May issue, visually highlighting their particular appeals. Their works' repeated inclusion in exhibitions and press alike reflected Evelyn and Jerry's reputation as designer-craftsmen who designed effectively across media.

The Ackermans' flexible approach to materials proved savvy in a market that demanded new patterns and product types regularly. Creatively adapting existing designs allowed them to expand their product line in a scalable fashion. Evelyn's signs of the *Zodiac*, for example, became one of her most popular designs, produced from 1958 until the early 1980s in various materials. While the *Zodiac* series initially came to market as 12 individual mosaics in shades of blue, green, and purple, in the very same year the Ackermans also used the design for a silk screen in the entirely different colorway of orange and red. The translation into print required reconsidering the same pattern with attention to negative space, which was necessitated by the stencil-based process of printing colors in layers. In 1964 Evelyn modified her *Zodiac* design yet again, this time for Panelcarve, the company started with Sherrill Broudy in 1963, now attending to the sculptural qualities of bas-relief wood carving. Each new product type required tailoring the idea to its intended medium, a process that allowed for the renewal of a singular design.

In the 1980s, as the Ackermans wound down their business, they each returned wholeheartedly to their own studio practices. While Jerry came full circle to focus once again on ceramics, Evelyn threw herself into perfecting the enameling technique of cloisonné. Such material curiosity and intimate connection to craftsmanship remained a constant in Evelyn's and Jerry's artistic lives; it was the thread that tied their work together over decades.

PREVIOUS PAGES The hand carving process was highlighted on the cover of a Forms+Surfaces catalog. OPPOSITE An assemblage of tools, cartoons, mosaic tiles, and color keys was photographed on Evelyn's drafting table. OVERLEAF TOP The heavy kraft paper *Flower Garden #206* mosaic template was drawn in pencil and labeled with numbers corresponding to tile colors and notes in Spanish for "claro" (clear) and "oscuro" (opaque). The mosaic artists chalked the back and then traced the outline on the front to transfer the design onto a Masonite backing. OVERLEAF BOTTOM On a full-size tissue drawing of *Flower Garden* overlaid on a grid, Evelyn indicated colors in colored pencil. PAGES 72–73 In a detail of the handwoven 20-by-60-inch *Flower Garden* tapestry, the jewel tones complement the abstracted floral and plant forms of the 1958 design.

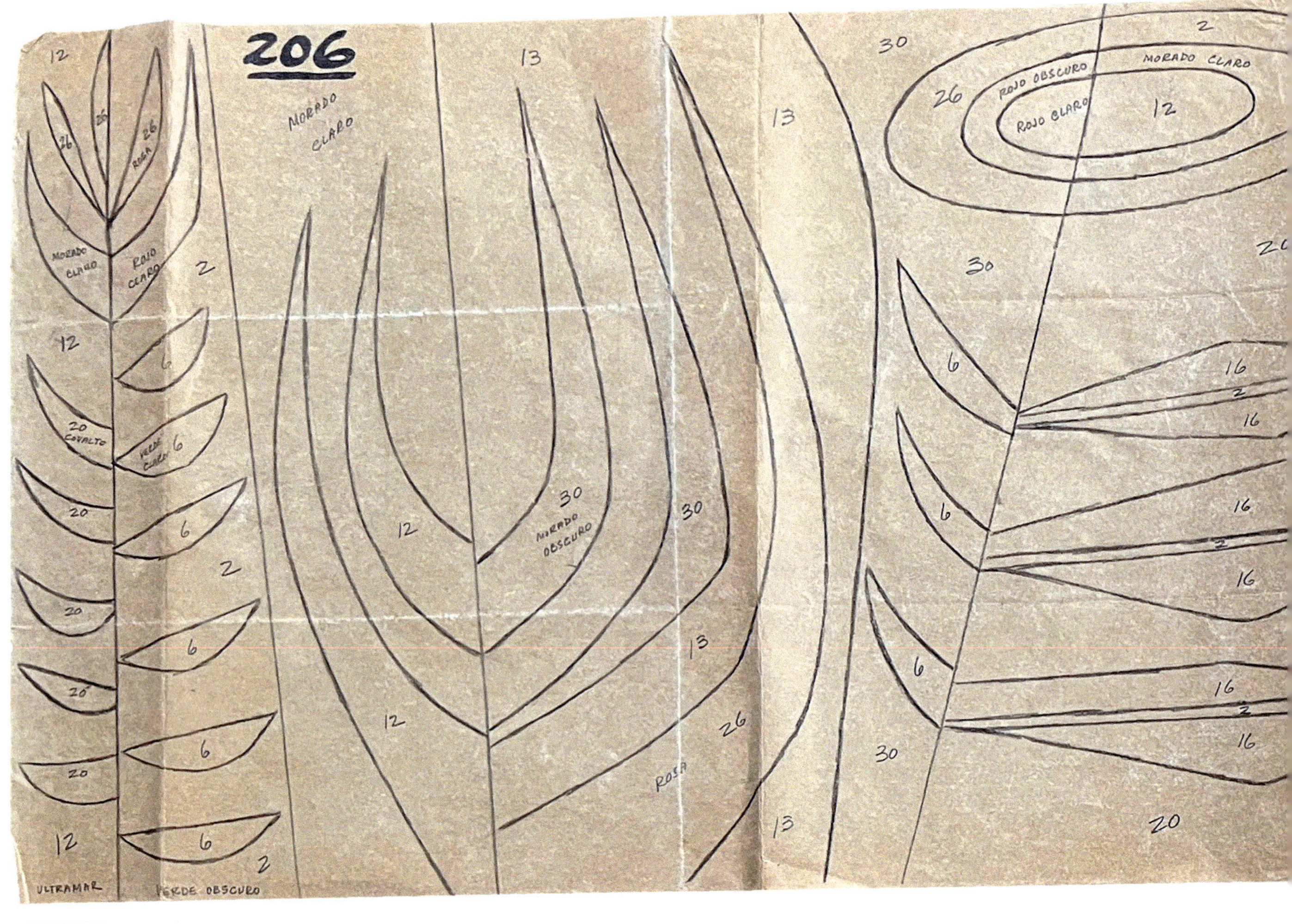
206
MORADO CLARO
ROJO OBSCURO
ROJO CLARO
MORADO OBSCURO
ROSA
COBALTO
VERDE CLARO
ULTRAMAR
VERDE OBSCURO

MORADO CLARO
ROJO CLARO
MORADO CLARO
ROJO CLARO
MORADO CLARO
MORADO CLARO

TOP A diminutive tissue paper concept of *Flower Garden* measures only 2⅜ by 9¾ inches. ABOVE Smaller than the handwoven tapestry, the 12-by-36-inch mosaic *Flower Garden* illustrates the effect of material on a design. The vibrant colors and simplified shapes are retained, but the texture and surface character of the mosaic introduce a different element.

ABOVE AND ABOVE RIGHT *Hot Bird* was Evelyn's first tapestry design and was handwoven in Mexico in 1957. While the tapestry measures 30 by 60 inches, the mosaic is 12 by 36 inches and is executed in slightly softer colors. OPPOSITE *Hot Bird* was featured on the cover of the *Los Angeles Times Home* magazine in 1957 as part of *California Design III*, along with Van Keppel-Green metal furniture, a Harrison McIntosh ceramic bowl, and a Gasper Peralta wood cup.

Six pages of new color and styling at the third California Design Exhibition

James Reed

See Page 10

James Reed See Page

OPPOSITE On January 12, 1958—Evelyn's 34th birthday—a *California Design IV* installation photograph appeared on the cover of the *Los Angeles Times Home* magazine. ABOVE *Knight on Horse* illustrates the Ackermans' experimentation with executing a single design across multiple media. Originally titled *Falconer*, the flat stylized depiction of a cloaked knight holding a falcon and astride a horse was produced as a 12-by-48-inch mosaic, *above right*, from 1957 to 1965 and a 24-by-65-inch tapestry, *above left*, from 1958 to 1968. When introduced, the mosaic retailed for $100 and the tapestry $70, reflecting the difference in production costs. While not commercially offered, the striking etched anodized black aluminum 12-by-39-inch panel, *above center*, because it lacks the saturated colors in the tapestry and mosaic, instead uses slight variations in pattern decoration to produce visual interest.

VIRGO

SCORPIO

GEMINI

OPPOSITE AND ABOVE Evelyn's *Zodiac* designs, first released in 1958 as individual 18-inch mosaics and a 52-by-38-inch linen silk-screened panel that included all of the 12 signs, became the basis for her 1964 Panelcarve design. Full-size drawings show the mosaics in various shades of blue and green while the silk screen was offered in warm and cool colorways, orange and red or blue and green, with a border incorporating all the zodiac symbols. In the 9-by 36-inch woodcarvings, a border motif fills space and frames the images. The tongue-and-groove system is visible at the top.

CERAMICS

JO LAURIA AND DALE CAROLYN GLUCKMAN

Jerry's first encounter with ceramics occurred after returning to Wayne University following World War II to continue his undergraduate education on the GI Bill. It was there that he visited Evelyn's ceramic class. Intrigued, he signed up for a course with John Foster, her instructor. Foster emphasized Chinese, Japanese, and Korean pottery and the work of Shoji Hamada and Bernard Leach. This exposure led Jerry to a lifelong love of ceramics, drawn to the tactile and three-dimensional qualities of shaping clay.

When Charles M. Harder, chairman of the New York State College of Ceramics at Alfred University, juried a senior art show at Wayne, he was impressed by Jerry's work and offered him a place in the Alfred MFA program. Jerry began his graduate studies in 1951, and his instructors Harder, Daniel Rhodes, and Marguerite Wildenhain influenced his approach to ceramic design and led him "to explore the spirit of clay and what could be done with a simple, honest approach to form, function, and decoration." On his hand-thrown pieces, Jerry's aesthetic frequently favored smooth matte glazes, often layered over other surface treatments.

Jerry and Evelyn had their individual and collaborative ceramics represented in prestigious national and regional exhibitions from 1951–1955, including, among many others the *Syracuse Ceramic National, Young Americans, Fiber-Clay-Metal,* and the *Smithsonian Kiln Club*. Regional exhibitions included the *Michigan Artist-Craftsman,* the Michigan State Fair, the *Scripps Invitational*, and the California State Fair. Jerry also had one-man exhibitions at Los Angeles venues, including UCLA in 1954. Early in their careers, the Ackermans received national recognition. *Ceramics Monthly*, the *Los Angeles Times Home* magazine, and other publications covered them along with other prominent ceramists of the time.

While establishing Jenev in 1953, Jerry put into practice the techniques and knowledge he had learned at Alfred University, including proficiency in clay bodies, kiln firing temperatures, and glaze calculation and development to achieve desired effects. His master's project was a chocolate pot created using the slip-cast method (an industrial technique of making multiples using liquid clay and molds). Ten Jenev pieces (including black-and-white, majolica, and sgraffito examples) were included in the *California Designed* exhibition at the Long Beach Municipal Art Center and the Oakland Art Museum in 1955. Seven Jenev ceramics were selected for the inaugural *California Design I* show in 1954–1955. The invitation to the exhibition explained the objectives, "Ranging in scope from a street sweeper to a cigarette cup, this exhibition brings credit and recognition to those designers, manufacturers, and retailers who have brought to the consumer excellence in design and function." A representative of the United States Information Agency in Washington, D.C., visited the *Designer-Craftsmen of the West, 1957* at the San Francisco M. H. De Young Memorial Museum and was so impressed with the quality of the material that part of the exhibition, including a Jenev vase and bowl, was selected for a two-year tour of Europe and the Near East.

The Ackermans marketed Jenev pieces as both decorative and functional; they were promoted in their brochures as "sensitive forms combined with soft, stoney matte glazes [that] produce pottery of the highest quality and elegance." As the line expanded, there were more than 20 forms offered in 10 different glaze and surface treatments, greatly increasing the variety of products without requiring the development of additional shapes. Some pieces were sold only briefly, including a small fish-shaped dish. The first pieces—in black or white or a combination of both—were soon joined by others decorated with stars and flowers in rust, blue, and green majolica glazes. Some pieces featured blue and white incised sgraffito or Mishima patterns.

A yellow glaze, as well as stripes in majolica turquoise and green or wax-resist blue and charcoal, were introduced in 1954. Not every shape was available in every glaze color and combination. While Evelyn's decorations, each drawn freehand onto the bisque piece, were figural, featuring attenuated kings and queens (available only on two products: trays and stoppered bottles), Jerome's were more graphic. Soon the Ackermans introduced pieces playfully named the "Fun Bird" group with simplified bird forms shaped into bowls, candleholders, and ashtrays. "I've always loved bird forms. They lend themselves to design beautifully," Jerry commented. To establish their company brand, a "JENEV" signature or "a Jenev design by Ackerman" was inscribed on the underside of the bases, sometimes with the model number.

As Jenev became ERA in late 1956 and that new venture grew, the Ackermans stopped making ceramics. It was 30 years before Jerry returned to the studio to work again in clay.

OPPOSITE Jerry took his first ceramics class from John Foster at Wayne University. Only 5¾ inches high, this early example is recorded in his notebook as "bisqued at cone 04 with a white slip pattern made up of kaolin, ball clay, buck spar, and flint with a wax resist." OVERLEAF LEFT *Vase with Female Figures* represented the Ackermans' first collaboration in 1952. Jerry threw the stoneware vessel and Evelyn drew the sgraffito decoration using Jerry's glazes. OVERLEAF RIGHT Jerry decorated his 11-inch-tall vase with a brown and black matte glaze and incised primitive sgraffito figures. One of his MFA pieces at Alfred University, the vase was shown at the *Ceramic National* in Syracuse and at *Wichita Decorative Arts*.

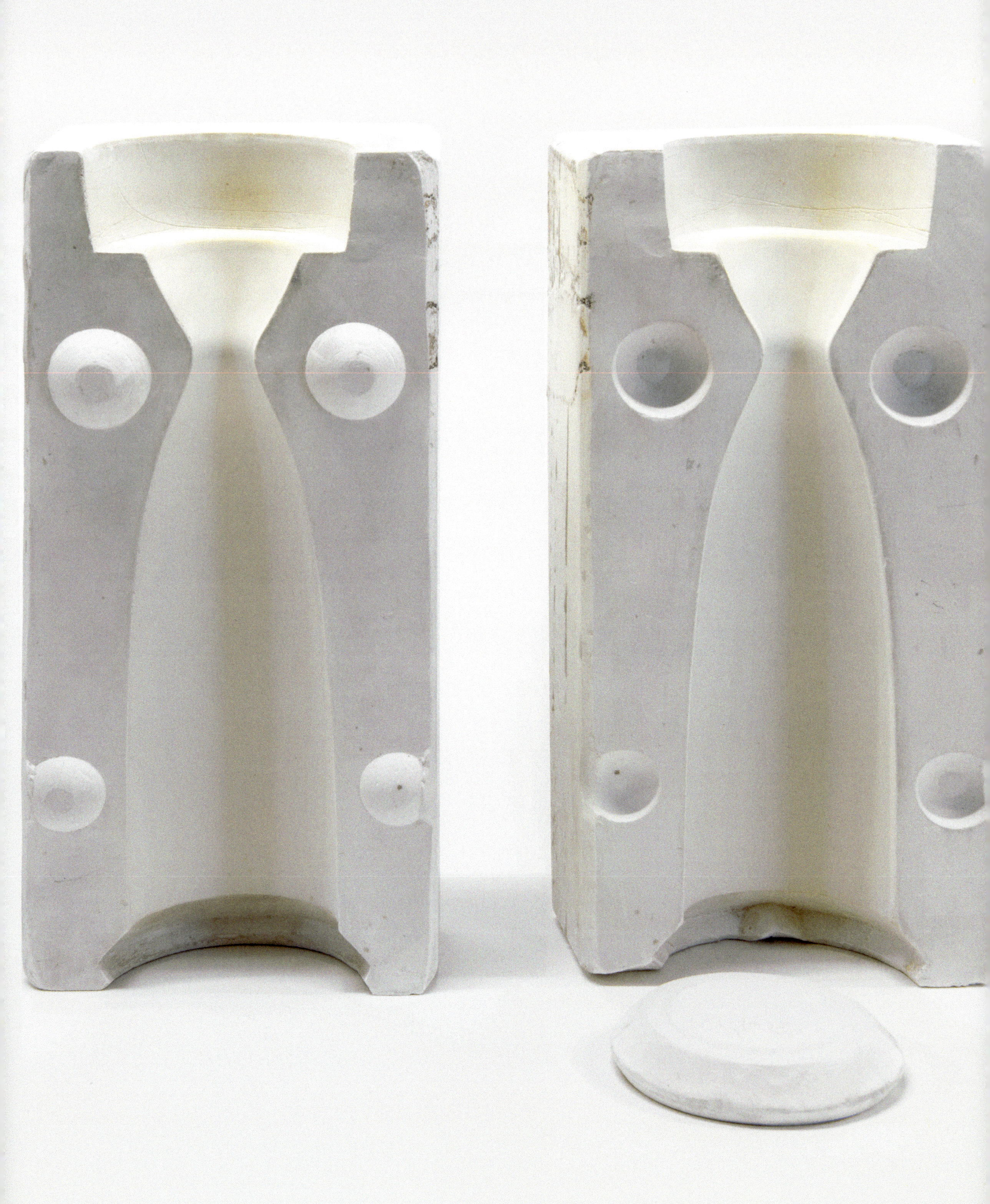

PREVIOUS PAGES Multiple steps were involved in creating the production molds for the Ackermans' Jenev slip-cast ceramics. After Jerry carved a plaster model, he created a master, which in turn was used to make the plaster molds. The 8½-inch-high #107 vase required a three-part mold because of the separate base, which included a "JENEV" inscription. The model, master, and molds were slightly oversized to allow for the shrinkage that occurred in the firing. ABOVE Sensitive forms combined with soft matte glazes were the hallmark of the Jenev ceramics. Jerry's black-and-white palette applied to the vase,

bottle, and bowl shapes and shown in this vintage promotional photograph from 1954, still feels modern more than 70 years later. Jenev pieces were exhibited in the 1955 *California Designed* and *California Design* shows. OVERLEAF A group of sleek earthenware vases, ranging in height from 8½ inches to 12½ inches high, and a fruit bowl that is 14 inches long, were designed and produced by Jerry in 1953 and reflect the influence of Charles M. Harder, Daniel Rhodes, and Marguerite Wildenhain on what he described as an "honest approach to form, function, and decoration."

PREVIOUS PAGES LEFT Jerry introduced a blue and deep charcoal color combination in 1954, experimenting with a white-matte glaze over a black glaze to produce the bold stripes on the bottle and coordinated wine cups as well as on vases and small bowls. PREVIOUS PAGES RIGHT Form and function pair in the 1954 14½-inch-high bottles with stoppers designed by Jerry and individually hand decorated by Evelyn with elongated queens and kings in the Mishima technique of inlaying slip, underglaze, or clay into a contrasting clay body. Retailing at $17 apiece, these were the most expensive of the Jenev products.

ABOVE A number of Jenev pieces were offered in a yellow glaze the Ackermans referred to as "golden ambrosia matte" including this scallop-edged 5½-by-9¾-inch bowl. OVERLEAF Wanting to try Jenev pieces in a different clay body, Jerry found a small company producing white stoneware and completed this set with a variegated brown and rust glaze. The stoneware, however, was ultimately never put into production.

TOP Bird bowls were part of the "Fun Bird" group that included candleholders and an ashtray introduced in 1954. They represent two of the glaze decoration approaches that Jerry often used—colorful majolica on the white version and incised linework on the black version. ABOVE Split by a subtle brown line where the black-and-white matte glazes overlap, the small bowl and covered jar, shown in *California Designed 1955* make a graphic statement. OPPOSITE Paul McCobb introduced Jenev ceramics to the national market—here displayed on the Living Wall—through his Directional showroom beginning in early 1954. McCobb's wife, Mary Frances Rogers, wrote that they were "very pleased with the way they . . . compliment [sic] our furniture designs."

MOSAICS

JO LAURIA AND DALE CAROLYN GLUCKMAN

As a result of Evelyn's deep interest in the long history and material of mosaics, the Ackermans added mosaic work to the Jenev product line in 1955. Evelyn made the mosaics herself, and they immediately proved to be popular products. As the Ackermans expanded Jenev and it transitioned into ERA Industries, the demand for their mosaic tables and wall panels also increased. Soon the labor-intensive nature of the work they were doing themselves necessitated finding a workshop where skilled artisans still practiced handcraftsmanship but were within a reasonable shipping distance to Los Angeles. To this end, they enlisted the assistance of Sherrill Broudy, who had joined ERA Industrias in 1956 and had spent considerable time in Mexico. Eventually, Broudy found an American agent who lived in Mexico and could help them source and manage the work.

They planned to start on a modest scale. Their agent located an empty storefront in Mexico City and hired one skilled mosaic artist, Maria Helena, to begin working on the Ackermans' designs. To facilitate communication, Evelyn would send a full-sized template drawing with instructions in Spanish and samples of the tile or color notations. The design was then transferred onto a Masonite backing by tracing the outline and the tiles glued onto it. In 1963 in an interview in *Interior Previews*, the Ackermans were quoted as stating that to their amazement "every day we found that Maria had another sister or brother working, too—at the end of two weeks, 30 of her relatives, probably her entire family, were working for ERA. It was obvious we had to sell mosaics."

That did not prove to be difficult. One of the largest customers for their mosaics was Chicago's Marshall Field department store. By 1958 Evelyn, liberated from the actual hands-on work, was able to expand the line to 54 designs now retailing for between $40 and $115. This represented a significant increase in both quantity and design variety. By 1964 ERA price lists reflected a selection of nearly 70 mosaic designs in the product line. Evelyn generally designed for 12-by-36-inch, 12-by-48-inch, and 12-by-60-inch rectangles and 18-inch rounds or squares. Standardizing the size of their mosaic panels reduced the cost of materials and thus lowered prices for their clients. The Venetian glass tesserae mosaic tiles were nevertheless handcut to fit the individual designs—this laborious process produced only one square foot of mosaic a day. The Ackermans followed a limited production model, ordering no more than six of each design at a time.

The *Milwaukee Journal* on December 15, 1957, referred to the collection as "long and lean of shape, some of which can be hung either horizontally or vertically" and noted that they were "done in currently popular home decorating colors—blues and greens or combinations of orange, beige, and yellow tones."

The mosaics were originally framed in metal, but the Ackermans changed to dark wood frames as a less-expensive option to produce and ship. When the first imported group arrived on Western Airlines, Jerry found that United States Customs had no identifier for that product type and labeled it "glass, other." Within a year, the Ackermans produced enough pieces that Customs created a specific category for mosaics.

Most of the designs were created in 1957 and 1958 and were in production for less than a decade. Several mosaics were joint collaborations between Evelyn and Jerry, such as the iconic *Elipses*, although *Autumn Abstract* was Jerry's design. The mosaics were available in a wide range of subject matter including geometrics, abstracts, and human, animal, and mythical motifs; as with many of their product offerings, numerous designs came in warm and cool colorways. The *California Design* exhibition series included eight ERA mosaics, beginning with *Mermaid* in 1957.

In addition to their line of individual mosaic panels, ERA also fulfilled architectural commissions for mosaics, including interior and exterior mosaics for Mammoth Mountain Inn and large custom panels for building exteriors. The first was *Fantasy Landscape*, for the facade of an apartment building by Broudy on Kiowa Avenue in West Los Angeles, made by Evelyn in their Jenev studio in Los Angeles. The next, *Land, Sea, and Sky* was designed for the architect Louis Mazzetti in 1957 for a professional building on East Victoria Street in Santa Barbara, California. These large installations were produced in segments then assembled onsite—for example, *Land, Sea, and Sky* was made in Mexico in 30 sections.

Mosaics were one of ERA's most successful design lines. However, after 1965 the Ackermans discontinued production of mosaic products when they discovered that their most popular designs were being copied by competitors.

OPPOSITE Evelyn designed the large 48-by-36-inch glass-tile *Rain* mosaic in a variation of a favorite motif. She worked with traditional Italian tesserae glass tiles to create overlapping colors and striking patterns in the active composition. The mosaic was the centerpiece of a contemporary kitchen in a Los Angeles penthouse designed by Cannell & Chaffin for Victor Carter, the president of the United Way and Republic Pictures, and his wife Adrea.

ABOVE A detail of a bird atop a plant in the mosaic mural *Fantasy Landscape*, designed by Evelyn in 1956 and now registered with the Los Angeles Mural Conservancy, displays the vibrant colors and intricate execution of the variously shaped tiles. OPPOSITE Evelyn posed under the scaffolding at the building site of the mural commissioned by their former partner architect Sherrill Broudy to complement the minimalist facade of an apartment building on Kiowa Avenue

in West Los Angeles. The *Los Angeles Times Home* magazine of March 3, 1957, described how "the playful gathering of birds and plant life gives the building an elegant note that adds immeasurably to its completeness." Because of its 22-foot height, it was necessary for Evelyn to fabricate the mosaic in three sections at the Jenev studio. The Ackermans effectively drew a connection between mosaic as a medium and public building adornment.

PREVIOUS PAGES *Cats*, measuring 45 by 20 by 14 inches, was one of the first mosaic-topped tables the Ackermans produced in 1955. The simplified forms in black, white, and grey porcelain tiles are accented with Italian red, orange, and gold glass tiles, backed with gold leaf, which create depth and richness. OPPOSITE A collaboration between Evelyn and Jerry in 1958, the 12-by 60-inch *Elipses* mosaic proved so successful that they introduced a warm version in 1960, and adapted the design to a hooking in 1970. ABOVE The Palmer & Krisel model home in the Pacifica Tract in San Diego, California, was built by the developer Leonard Drogin in 1961. The mosaic was paired with a Vista of California table to complement the interior in this image by Julius Shulman.

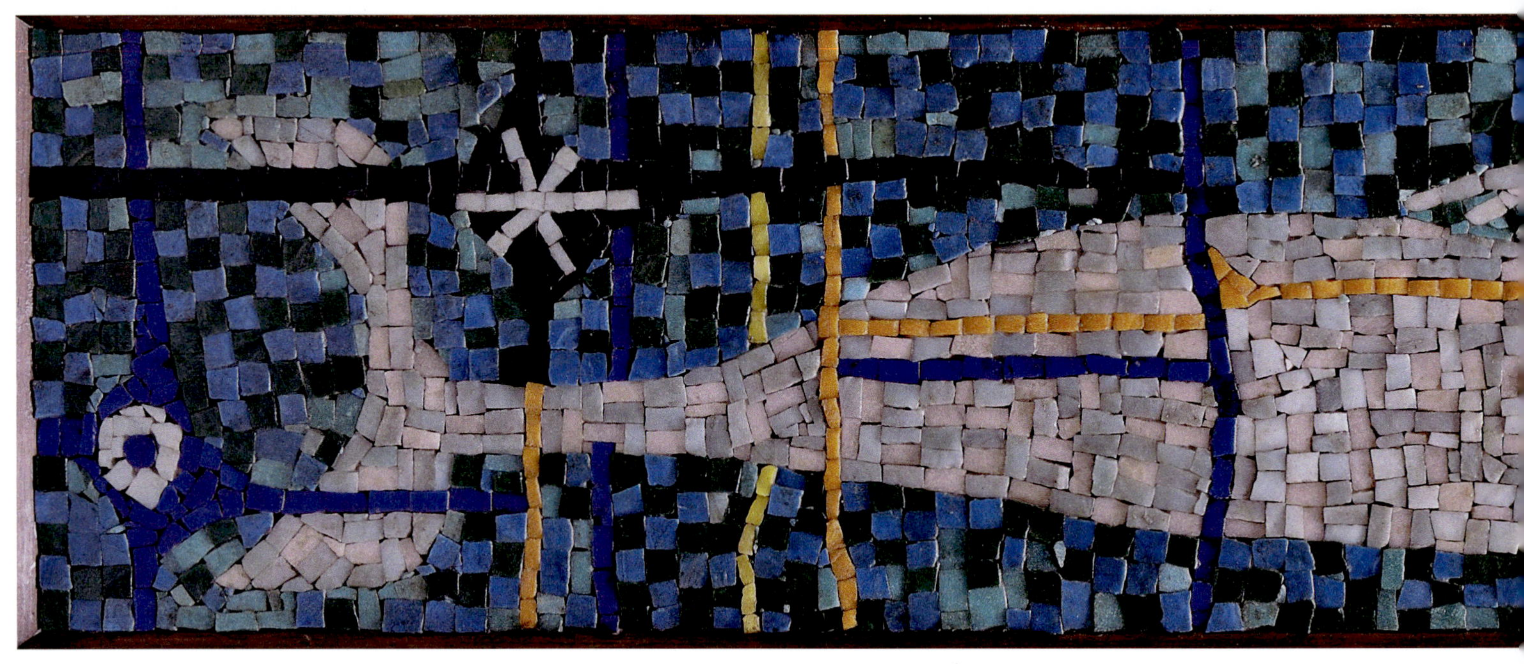

TOP Whether hung horizontally or vertically, the rhythmic visual progression of the cool 12-by-60-inch *Elipses* mosaic is enhanced by the natural variation in the glass tiles, which imbue a depth and dimension that flat colors lacked. It was exhibited in *California Design IV.* ABOVE Within the narrow, long composition that is constrained by the 12-by-60-inch size, Evelyn created a sense of movement and flow with a graceful mermaid gazing out at the viewer from the sea. It was the first mosaic to be included in *California Design III* in 1957. This piece would have taken the mosaic artisans at least five days to execute.

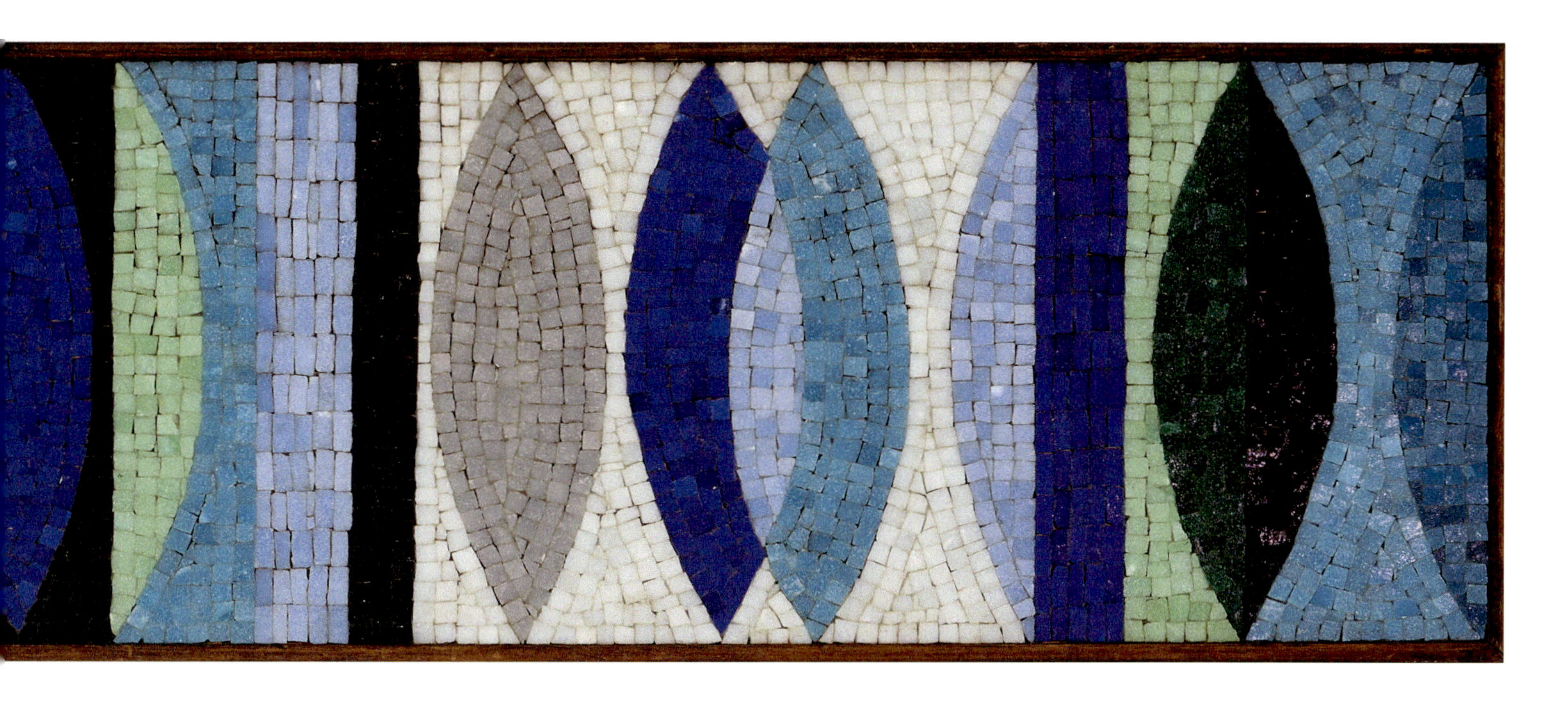

ABOVE Recalling a city skyline, the geometric 12-by-48-inch *Fachada* mosaic uses repeated forms of triangles, squares, and rectangles transformed into a vibrant grid because of Evelyn's eye for color and the variations created by the tiles themselves, many set in a basketweave pattern.

TOP AND ABOVE *Pennants* was the only mosaic to be offered in three lengths—12 inches high by 36, 48, and 60 inches long, with all sizes available in a blue and green or orange and yellow color combination, demonstrating how the Ackermans adapted a single design to create six different products. The warm and cool colorways of the 12-by-48-inch design illustrate the effect of color on the overall appearance of the piece. OVERLEAF A detail of the 60-inch *Pennants*

mosaic reveals the complexity and skill required to cut the tiles with tile nippers to fit the shapes as well as the variety of patterns created by the shapes and placement of the square and rectangular tiles. The circle and diamond design of the 60-and 36-inch mosaics differed slightly from the 48-inch size.

ABOVE LEFT In 1958 Jerry designed *Autumn Abstract* and worked with Evelyn to determine the color palette of this mosaic which was included in *California Design IV.* Later, the Ackermans adapted the 12-by-48-inch design as a hooked wall hanging. The overlapping "H" shapes utilize different colors at the intersections. ABOVE RIGHT The white "tortilla" tiles that form the woman's dress in the *San Blas* mosaic were made in Mexico by pouring molten glass into flat molds, which were cooled and then shattered, resulting in odd-shaped pieces and sizes. This 12-by-36-inch design from 1959 echoes themes from a

custom installation for Cannell & Chaffin. ABOVE LEFT The 1959 Puerta mosaic represented a 12-by-48-inch stylized door. ABOVE RIGHT Although in a different color scheme and in a smaller 12-by-48-inch size than the *Hot Summer* Landscape tapestry, the *Clouds* mosaic, produced from 1959 to 1965, retained the same biomorphic elements.

ABOVE *Byzantia*, a compact 12-by-36-inch mosaic, evokes a brightly colored, crowded Middle Eastern city compressed into a stacked composition. Entirely self-taught, Evelyn was inspired by an exhibition of mosaics she had seen in San Francisco. This was the only mosaic exhibited in *California Designed.*
OPPOSITE LEFT Designed to be flexible enough to be hung on the wall either horizontally or vertically, *Adhara Abstract*, measuring 12 by 60 inches, employs

simple but vibrant geometric stripes and rectangles and was shown in *California Design V.* ABOVE RIGHT The aptly named *Kiowa Abstract* mosaic from 1957, measuring 12 by 60 inches, combined brightly colored geometric patterns and abstracted floral shapes in a bold modernist design.

ABOVE Evelyn made a *Partridge* mosaic for her mother. Set in a metal frame, the mosaic has a white tile at the bottom of the bird with a tiny "Ackerman" inscribed. When the mosaic production was moved to Mexico, the Ackermans ceased the use of porcelain and gilt tiles. The gilt foil-backed tiles were expensive and difficult to get, so Evelyn shifted the colors to work with the imported Italian tiles available in Mexico. OPPOSITE A series of three 12-by-36-inch mosaics designed in 1957—*Partridge*, *Hot Bird*, and *Bird*—could be hung separately or as a group. Only *Partridge* was included in *California Design IV*. The forward-facing *Bird* employed the same depiction of tail feathers and a similar color palette as *Hot Bird*, which was designed in profile. OVERLEAF With its gold-leaf tiles and complex design, Evelyn's handmade 1956 *Young Warrior* mosaic prototype was simplified for later production in Mexico.

PREVIOUS PAGES LEFT Designed in 1957 for a Louis Mazzetti office building at 112 East Victoria Street, a detail of the *Sea, Land, and Sky* mosaic reflects the beach atmosphere of Santa Barbara, California. Because of its size, the mural was executed at the ERA atelier in Mexico in 30 sections. PREVIOUS PAGES RIGHT The final colored-pencil cartoon was one of several color variations Evelyn explored. ABOVE AND OPPOSITE In 1958 and 1959, Evelyn designed nine

18-inch round mosaics that included *Horse, Owl, Rooster, Mermaid, Greek God, Greek Goddess*, and *Girl and Bird*. Unlike the larger mosaics, the circular mosaics had wood backs and brass frames. At their introduction, designs C-02 *Jester* and C-01 *Girl with Lyre* each retailed for $50.

HANDWOVEN TAPESTRIES

DALE CAROLYN GLUCKMAN AND JO LAURIA

Evelyn's abiding interest in textiles began in 1941 at the University of Michigan when she took a weaving class and fell in love with the tactile quality of handwoven fabric. In 1957 Jerry and Evelyn decided to introduce woven hangings to complement their existing line of silk screens. They found a group of skilled weavers outside Mexico City who produced traditional wool serapes and could adapt to their requirements. Evelyn's bold designs and bright colors were a departure for the weavers, who nevertheless embraced them.

The 1957 *Hot Bird*, Evelyn's first tapestry, was followed by nearly 100 more over the next 20 years. A July 1958 price list includes 11 handwoven tapestry designs retailing from $60 to $90. By 1963 there were 27, and in 1970 there were nearly 60 tapestries available (although some were colorway alternatives).

As with the mosaics, the number of skilled handweavers started small and grew as family members joined the workshop. The Ackermans engaged an American business agent they knew in Mexico to find and start off the workshops, but ultimately the couple worked directly with the weavers. The workshops were family-based, and, in the case of the Gueveras, with whom they worked the longest, when the father retired, the daughter took over. The relationship with these small multigenerational workshops was very personal.

A letter accompanying their 1965 catalog states "The handweaving of tapestries is a painstaking process, requiring weeks of work for each one. The homespun wools are hand-dyed in colors that are as brilliant as the Mexican sun. The tapestries are characterized by the festive, rich color-scale and a flat weave. This is part of ERA's own program of seeking skilled craftsmen and developing a design program to put their talents to work."

Evelyn started with small concept drawings, and when they decided to move forward with a design, she projected it on a wall to enlarge it to the desired size, traced it on paper, and attached colors keyed to yarn samples, especially if the design was to be produced in multiple colorways. The weavers followed Evelyn's full-sized drawings and detailed instructions. This ensured consistency, although given their handmade nature, no two tapestries were identical. For *Birds of a Feather*, Evelyn emphasized, "The design must be followed accurately. Crispness is important to the concept," and asked the agent to translate her instructions into Spanish. The agent in Mexico City was close enough to drive the drawings to the workshop and review them. Evelyn stressed that colors were to match the yarns and not the "crayon" (colored pencil she used to indicate color). To achieve the rich, saturated colors that Evelyn specified, they ordered dyes from Germany.

Once dyed, the yarn was woven on simple looms that limited the size of flat-weave pieces that could be produced. It was only in 1969 that a larger loom became available, and four tapestries in the maximum 44-by-70-inch size were added in 1970, including *Launch Pad* and *Aerial View*. Few weavers could produce the fine quality required—if they left or retired, they were difficult to replace because individual weavers often specialized in a particular design. Once completed, a sample of each new design was sent to Evelyn and Jerry for approval. The cost was determined by square meter of wool, and the Ackermans guaranteed the workshop in Mexico a monthly order. They followed a limited production model, ordering small quantities so that the designs would not be overproduced.

Between 1959 and 1963 the Ackermans briefly experimented with handweaving tapestries in Italy, where they already had their hardware made, but it proved to be too expensive. They also investigated engaging Walter and Bundy Illsley, who lived Mexico and worked with Alexander Girard.

Interiors magazine announced in 1970 "Era Industries, Inc. weaves its way into the new decade with hand-hooked and handwoven tapestries of geometric designs and abstracted shapes in lush colors or black, white, and gray. Their titles are as intriguing as the designs." Popular designs were made for a decade or more. *Spring Birds* and *Flower Pot*, introduced in 1959, were sold until 1982; *Canal* and *Cat and Bird* were produced from 1962 to 1982. *Canal* exemplifies how a complex color palette could be translated into both warm and cool tones. The small *Arbole* introduced in 1964 was so successful that in 1970 a larger size was added. Nonetheless, some designs or color options had a life-span of only a few years. If a colorway or design did not sell, it was discontinued—for example, the orange and yellow *Op 66* was sold long after other colors were dropped.

Ultimately, the tapestries met Evelyn's expressed goal "to design things with character that were well made." The Ackermans created more than 60 different designs over the years, and many were produced in more than one colorway, which gave customers an extensive selection of tapestries from which to choose.

OPPOSITE While on an airplane flight, Jerry was inspired by the landscape he saw below, which led him to design *Aerial View*. Measuring 44-by-70-inches, the 1970 pattern was the largest size available in the tapestry line. The *San Francisco Chronicle* remarked that "Evelyn Ackerman took honors for a group of wool tapestries woven in Mexico in bold free form designs," referencing *California Design XI* that included *Aerial View*, as well as *Launch Pad*, *Labyrinth*, *Blocks*, and *Campesina*.

E
A

LOS ANGELES TIMES
May 3, 1964
Home
COLORFUL SIMPLICITY IN A PAVILION HOUSE
Brilliant stylings in silk
ART FROM AFRICA
All-year garden color
Calorie-counting entrees
BARBECUE ROUND-UP
Glamorous game birds
Richard Fish

PREVIOUS PAGES LEFT The many tapestries Evelyn and Jerry produced over the years held to their credo of creating "handcrafted works of art of distinctive design, warmth, and texture." Designed in 1958 the *Hot Summer Landscape* tapestry in a palette of pink, orange, and red, was a striking 28-by-63-inch composition of biomorphic forms. PREVIOUS PAGES RIGHT The architect Richard Dorman not only designed the house overlooking Beverly Hills featured on the *Los Angeles Times Home* magazine cover of May 3, 1964, but also assisted with the interior design, mixing Eero Saarinen furniture, family heirlooms, and *Hot Summer Landscape*, which was shown in *California Design VII*. ABOVE To reduce expenses, the Ackermans altered the design and decreased the size of

Autumn Trees to one square meter of wool, measuring approximately 39 inches. Listed as "Tapis 714 chico, pura lana" on a 1958 invoice, the less complex version cost 175 pesos instead of 225 pesos to produce. The shapes were simplified, the gridded squares of the original were replaced by fewer scattered ones, and the number of colors was reduced from eight to five. ABOVE The original, slightly larger handwoven *Autumn Trees* tapestry represented fall foliage in an abstracted forest of trunks and leaves. The eight different yarn colors, irregular outlines, and numerous small squares in yellow, ochre, and burnt orange made the design more complex, and it took longer to weave.

ABOVE *Goat and Bull* could be purchased in a 45-by-21-inch size and as two separate tapestries. The simple forms in flat gold, black, and ivory from the 1969 composition define the bull with a horizontal line and the goat with vertical lines. OVERLEAF LEFT A strong shape and pattern are features of the 1965 *Stallion* tapestry, which measured 30 by 42 inches. OVERLEAF RIGHT Handwoven in Italy, where the heavy yarns were raised and the hemp backing was

exposed to create depth, *Stallion* was ultimately too expensive to produce there and weavers were becoming increasingly difficult to source, so the tapestry production was moved to Mexico instead.

PREVIOUS PAGES Moving seamlessly between styles, Evelyn portrayed a fanciful cityscape in *Buildings*, a 50-by-33-inch handwoven wool tapestry exhibited in *California Design IX*. ABOVE Blocks of color, including punchy tangerine, lemon, and tomato, define *Bell Tower*, designed in 1969 and measuring 22 by 48 inches. OPPOSITE Not only was the *Arbole* tapestry offered in different color combinations, including blue and green, yellow and green, orange and blue, and orange and tan, but the original smaller 23-by-35-inch size (also shown in *California Design IX*) was later made as a 44-by-70-inch version.

EA

EA

PREVIOUS PAGES LEFT Named for the year of its design, *Op 66* combined a series of blocks and stripes available in five color palettes. Exhibited in *California Design X*, the 24-by-72-inch design could be hung vertically or horizontally. PREVIOUS PAGES RIGHT Inspired by Neil Armstrong's 1969 moonwalk, the abstract *Moonscape* was produced as a 24-by-57-inch tapestry in vibrant pink, yellow, and orange, as well as earthtones of brown, black, and rust. ABOVE Harkening

back to the shapes of the 1959 *Forest* hooking, this much-simplified 23-by-44-inch handwoven *Forest* tapestry hit the market in 1977. ABOVE One of the smallest woven tapestries at 17 by 30 inches, *Noon* presents balanced compositional planes. The circles and curvilinear shapes were always a challenge to execute, and the skilled weavers in Mexico were able to keep edges smooth with a tight weave.

EA

EA

PREVIOUS PAGES LEFT With petals presented like a pinwheel on their stalk, the *Blossom* tapestry appears at once flat and beveled thanks to the alternating colors. The 1972 23-by-42-inch design was also offered with a blue flower. PREVIOUS PAGES RIGHT The lollipoplike blooms of *Flower Pot* from 1959 kept this charming small 23-by-32-inch tapestry in production from 1959 until 1982. Evelyn's joyous designs reflected her talent for composition, color, and shape.

OPPOSITE AND ABOVE *Striped Candy Tree* was produced between 1968 and 1972. The 26-by-46-inch handwoven tapestry was available in ochre and black, orange and yellow, and yellow and blue. Evelyn, in one of her more graphic tapestries, creates an abstract representation of a tree with offset lines and stacked shapes. The white cotton ERA labels were accidentally sewn on the front of these tapestries.

ABOVE AND OPPOSITE *Launch Pad* was one four designs produced in 1970 that maximized the loom capacity for 44-by-70-inch tapestries. Its graphic geometric design, inspired by the lift-off of the Apollo 11 rocket, combined with its large size made a bold impact, giving it a strong enough presence to serve as the focal point of a room and complement the Marcel Breuer *Wassily* chairs and Warren Platner side tables. OVERLEAF The abstract design of Evelyn's 1969 *Labyrinth* tapestries made in handwoven wool, each measuring 29 by 48 inches, changed according to the individual color schemes—from bold and striking in crisp black and ivory, *overleaf left*, to warm and soft in gradations of red, orange, and yellow, *overleaf right*.

ABOVE Composed of flat planes of strong color, *Campesina*, a 23-by-41-inch handwoven wool tapestry, depicts a simplified female figure holding a bowl of fruit. It was a best-seller and remained in the ERA line from 1969 through the 1980s. OPPOSITE Due to the popularity of the image inspired by Mexican peasants, Evelyn designed two more related tapestries including *Campesina 2* in 1972 to create a triptych. OVERLEAF LEFT *Woman with Basket*, while a different size at 19 by 48 inches, retained the colors and flavor of the *Campesina* tapestries, this time in profile. OVERLEAF RIGHT The composition of the *Cat and Bird* wool tapestry, which measures 23 by 45 inches, carries the eye in an upward direction from the flower in the bottom corner to the tail of the bird in the tree. After initially weaving the design in Italy, the Ackermans decided to produce it in Mexico.

EA

ER

ABOVE AND OPPOSITE The compact *Morning Dove*, 23 by 24 inches, designed in 1966, was sold in black and gold, orange and yellow, and blue and olive green versions. Evelyn's tapestries were often pictured in magazines with a focus on architecture and design: *Morning Dove* appeared on the cover of

Sunset magazine in October 1967. In 1973 a silk-screen adaptation was commissioned for the rooms in the Hyatt Hotel at Broadway Plaza in downtown Los Angeles that was designed by Charles Luckman Associates, the firm that developed Madison Square Garden arena in New York.

OPPOSITE AND ABOVE *Mother and Child*, a 16-by-45-inch handwoven wool tapestry, was designed in 1962 and shown in *California Design VIII*. In *Better Homes & Gardens* it is framed and hanging on the fireplace of a Palmer & Krisel home in the Drogin Company development of Del Cerro in San Diego, California. OVERLEAF A detail of the 1960 *Birds of a Feather* tapestry, reveals the geometric patterns within the abstract bird forms. Included in *California Design VII*, its 60-by-20-inch horizontal orientation made it ideal for hanging over a sofa.

TOP The 10-inch drawing for *Checkerboard* maintains a remarkable fidelity to the finished tapestry. Colors are keyed to yarn numbers. ABOVE *Checkerboard*, which was designed in 1959, is one of the few tapestries that was predominantly black. Although the 23-by-57-inch tapestry was also offered with an ivory background, the dark background presents a striking contrast to the vibrant colors of the line figures and pink and orange checks.

ABOVE The 1958 *King* tapestry, could be hung alone or with the 24-by-72-inch *Queen*. The pair were exhibited in *California Design VI* in 1960, with a group of Evelyn's rugs, and featured in the *Los Angeles Times Home* magazine that year. OPPOSITE This elegantly staged photograph by Julius Shulman from the *Los Angeles Times Home* magazine, captures Arthur Elrod's interior design for architects Palmer & Krisel's post-and-beam house built by Alexander Construction Company in Palm Springs, California. The *Queen* tapestry picks up the "rich, golden, uniquely right for the West" yellow of the room. Edward Frank used this tapestry, one of the many Ackerman designs he sold at Frank Brothers, in his Case Study House 25 by Killingsworth, Brady & Smith.

OPPOSITE The dramatic colorway of these *King* and *Queen* tapestries were introduced several years after the warm version. Production of the cool colors ceased by 1969, while the warm pair continued to be produced until 1979. Some of the dyes, including the purples, were prone to fading despite the Ackermans' best efforts to ensure colorfastness. ABOVE Evelyn's exposure to a wide variety of artistic expressions, from the work of the French artist Henri Matisse to so-called primitive art, is evident in the slender *Girl with Flowers*, 20 by 72 inches, an early 1958 design featured in *California Design V*.

EA

PREVIOUS PAGES The *Canal* tapestry in its cool colorway, a detail of which is shown here, was rendered in jewellike blue, purple, green, and magenta and demonstrates the quality of the weaving that the Ackermans were able to achieve. Evelyn tucked her EA initials into the steps leading out of the water.

ABOVE The 1962 *Canal*, a warm version measuring 60 by 20 inches, evoked the waterways of Venice, Italy, surrounded by densely packed representations of buildings. Both of the colorways were shown in *California Design VIII* and included in the educational filmstrips that accompanied the exhibition.

HOOKED RUGS AND HANGINGS

DALE CAROLYN GLUCKMAN AND JO LAURIA

In the late 1950s, Evelyn experimented with the hand-hooking technique popularly used for wool rugs. In 1959 shortly after introducing handwoven tapestries to their line, the Ackermans added hooked rugs and hangings to the ERA offerings, which they had handmade in Japan. Through a series of contacts, they found the Toyo Rug Company, Ltd., a small manufacturer based in Osaka, Japan, that had opened an office in downtown Los Angeles. Prices in Japan were reasonable, and the Ackermans found the manufacturers dependable, the quality high, and the production model well established. However the Ackermans' designs were nothing like the manufacturer had seen before.

With designs such as *Seed Pods* and *Pathways*, originally created as rugs, these textural pieces proved to be one of the most successful ERA product lines. Between 1959 and 1970, Evelyn created 75 hooked designs—135 with colorway variations. Some designs were produced for only a few years, while others, like the highly popular *Sun & Lion*, *Pheasant*, *Horse*, *Girl with Flowers*, *Girl with Birdcage*, *Monkeys*, *Skip Rope*, *Garden*, and *Wedding*, enjoyed long lifespans. Several designs were based on ERA mosaics, including Jerry's *Autumn Abstract* and their popular collaboration, *Elipses*.

In 1959 their ERA Industries catalog trumpeted, "An outstanding new series of colorful tapestry area rug designs by Evelyn Ackerman . . . an interesting accent on the floor to enhance the room or a wall hanging of incomparable beauty and texture." The handcrafted rugs were sold in a 3-by-5-foot size, with other sizes available. Soon realizing they were not equipped to compete in the overcrowded and highly competitive contemporary rug market, the Ackermans shifted their production to smaller wall hangings using the same technique. It was a logical transition: they visualized what could go in a Joseph Eichler or Harold Levitt house, and they found a ready market.

The 1959 price lists referenced "Tapestry-Rugs" that could be used on the floor or on the wall and, because of their wool content and latex backing, were durable. They soon referred to the pieces as "Hand-Hooked Tapestries" and "Tapestry Rugs" in one category and finer "Hand-Hooked Needlepoint Tapestries" in another. Over the next three years, the Ackermans introduced 27 different hand-hooked designs—46 in warm and cool colorways. By 1965 the number reached 48, totaling 80 items with color variations. The designs included abstracts, although many hooked hangings were more figural—depicting children, women, kings, and queens. Some were oriented toward more traditional interiors with heraldic and floral motifs. Others were more contemporary—like the Op Art *Stained Glass*. In *California Design VI* in 1960, four of the first designs were included: *Equestrian*, *Venetian Dusk*, *Sun Face*, and *Diamonds*.

Each piece was comprised of thousands of individual loops. The hooking technique places wool yarn on the back of a piece of coarsely woven fabric and draws small, even loops through the openings of the weave using a handheld hooking tool. The long or short size of the loop and whether or not it was cut allowed for variations in texture and depth, as seen in the *Garden* hooking.

As with the handwoven tapestries, a full-sized template and color key were supplied to ensure the accuracy of execution. Evelyn called out faces and curved areas for careful attention, smaller stitches, or thinner yarn. Colors were keyed to the yarns at the manufacturer; again, many of the designs were offered in warm and cool colorways. She referenced Tempo-Asia yarn colors numerically and reminded the suppliers to match the yarn colors rather than the color of the pencil in her drawing, specifying "color is to be clear and bright." Cost was calculated by the square foot; in 1968 it was $1.18 per square foot; by 1972 cost had risen to $2.20 per square foot.

To hold the yarn loops in place, the back was sprayed with latex, and while earlier pieces had a cotton backing, most simply had the raw edges finished on the back, turned over, and sewed down, leaving the latex back exposed. The hooked pieces were heavier than the handwoven tapestries, so the Ackermans used a simple tab system with a walnut-stained wood bar that slid through them for hanging. The tabs, initially hooked to match the wall hanging, were glued and sewn at the top for stability. As a cost-saving measure, later pieces had tabs in nylon/cotton tape sewn to the back.

The Ackermans experimented again with one of the last 1970 designs, *California Poppies*. They took the hooked version and produced it in Kashmir, India, as a crewel embroidery. The piece, emblematic of the Golden State, was included in *California Design '76*, the last of these shows.

OPPOSITE *Skip Rope*, with its idiosyncratic, compact depiction of a boy, avoids being sentimental or sweet. Hand hooked in Japan in 1961, its 24-by-36-inch size was relatively small. The EA initials, generally present on Evelyn's textiles, were sometimes omitted or, as in this case, appear backward. OVERLEAF LEFT The variation of cut loops and longer loops against the tight loop of the background, added tactile dimensionality that can be seen in the detail of *Garden*. OVERLEAF RIGHT In her hookings, Evelyn married a sophisticated sense of design with whimsy, creating pieces that were playful but not frivolous as in the hand-hooked *Garden*, a 23-by-32-inch wall hanging designed in 1962.

ABOVE AND OPPOSITE The *California Poppies* hooking, shown with its prepatory drawing, was on view in *California Design '76* and represented the distinctive character of California modernism, with its warm colors, intricate textures, and organic forms. This sample was an experimental version executed by skilled artisan embroiderers in Kashmir, India, but the commercially produced 39-by-35-inch pieces were hand hooked in Japan. OVERLEAF LEFT Savvy about the interiors market, the Ackermans knew that some designs, such as the 1959 *Sun & Lion*, a 36-by-60-inch "tapestry-rug" that coordinated with traditional and

contemporary settings, would be successful. The hooking married a medieval lion motif with a Mexican sun face. OVERLEAF RIGHT In 1970 Evelyn designed *Sun & Lioness*, a similar hooking in the heraldic theme, which measures 34 by 54 inches. While the treatment of the smiling sun and lioness shares the warm color palette, it feels very much of its time.

EA

ABOVE AND OPPOSITE Among the first hookings executed in Japan, the 1959 *Girl with Birdcage* and *Girl with Flowers*, each measuring 16 by 48 inches, reflect one of Evelyn's recurring motifs and the ability to play with pattern. These popular designs were sold through furniture, design, and department stores such as Barker Brothers, Leslie's, J. L. Hudson, Macy's, and Neiman Marcus. OVERLEAF The 1962 *Twilight Zone* episode "Cavender Is Coming" stars Jesse White as the apprentice angel Harmon Cavender and Carol Burnett as the unemployed Agnes Grep. Cavender consults his notes in Agnes' modest apartment, which is decorated with *Girl with Flowers*. The Ackermans' work was frequently used in television and movie set design, and this piece also appeared in a 2012 "Got Milk?" advertisement with Salma Hayek as well as in a 1999 episode of *Freaks and Geeks*.

ΣA

ΣA

TOP Evelyn deftly penciled in representative areas of color in an 8¼-by-3¼-inch drawing for *Forest* that keys to the cool yarn colors along the top and warm colors along the bottom to the yarns in Japan. ABOVE The stylized, bell-shaped trees in the hooking reflect Evelyn's sense of color, pattern, and form. The domestic scale of 48 by 18 inches and choice of color palette would have made it easy to place in a home in 1959 when it was designed.

ABOVE A roller coaster of spheres and spirals, *Stained Glass*, designed in 1967, juxtaposes riotous pink, orange, red, and ochre, or turquoise, cobalt, marine blue, olive green, and ochre in contrast to the cream neutral in these two 49-by-40-inch hookings. OPPOSITE The Ackermans' willingness to accommodate customer needs and offer different colorways to decorators broadened the appeal of their products. Color tests for the 1961 *Abstract No. 1* highlight the difference in contrast and feel of the colors, but the texture of the hooked wool loop created a warmth and softness despite the abstract nature of the design.

ABOVE Playful monkeys frolic on branches in this 1961 *Monkeys* hooking that was exhibited in *California Design VIII* in 1962. The 19-by-50-inch design embodies a Japanese ukiyo-e aesthetic in its elongated pictorial format, asymmetrical composition, ample empty space, and charming decorative motifs.

ABOVE The only hooking produced with tassels, *100 Plus*—which came in red, burgundy, and pink as well as this mustard, orange, red, and tan version —was only produced from 1967 to 1971. The hooked tabs for hanging match the color and technique of the background in this 24-by-38-inch piece. OPPOSITE Originally produced in Mexico as a handwoven tapestry, *Windows Abstract* was rereleased from 1970 to 1972 as a 20-by-59-inch hooking.

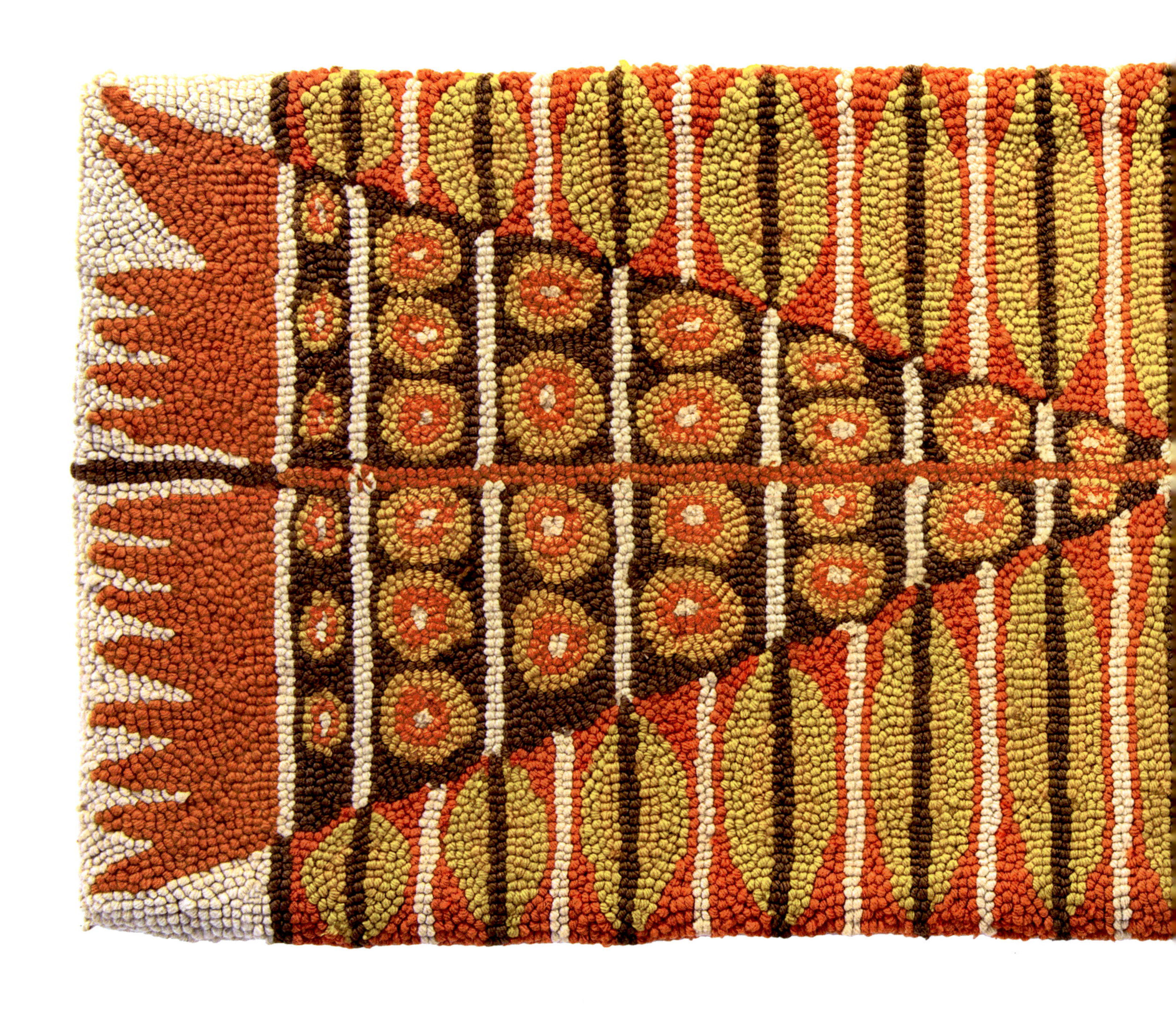

ABOVE An early "tapestry rug" design, the fanciful 48-by-18-inch *Plumage* depicts an imaginary bird and was offered in warm and cool versions. It is not a surprise that some of the patterns on the body and tail of the bird look similar to the *Forest* hooking since they were both designed in 1959. OVERLEAF The

regal 1959 *Pheasant* hooking, measuring 36 by 24 inches, was offered in oranges and browns or blues and greens. It was often paired with *Horse*, designed with the same border in 1959 and specified for the rooms at the Islandia Hotel built in 1961 in Mission Bay, California.

EA

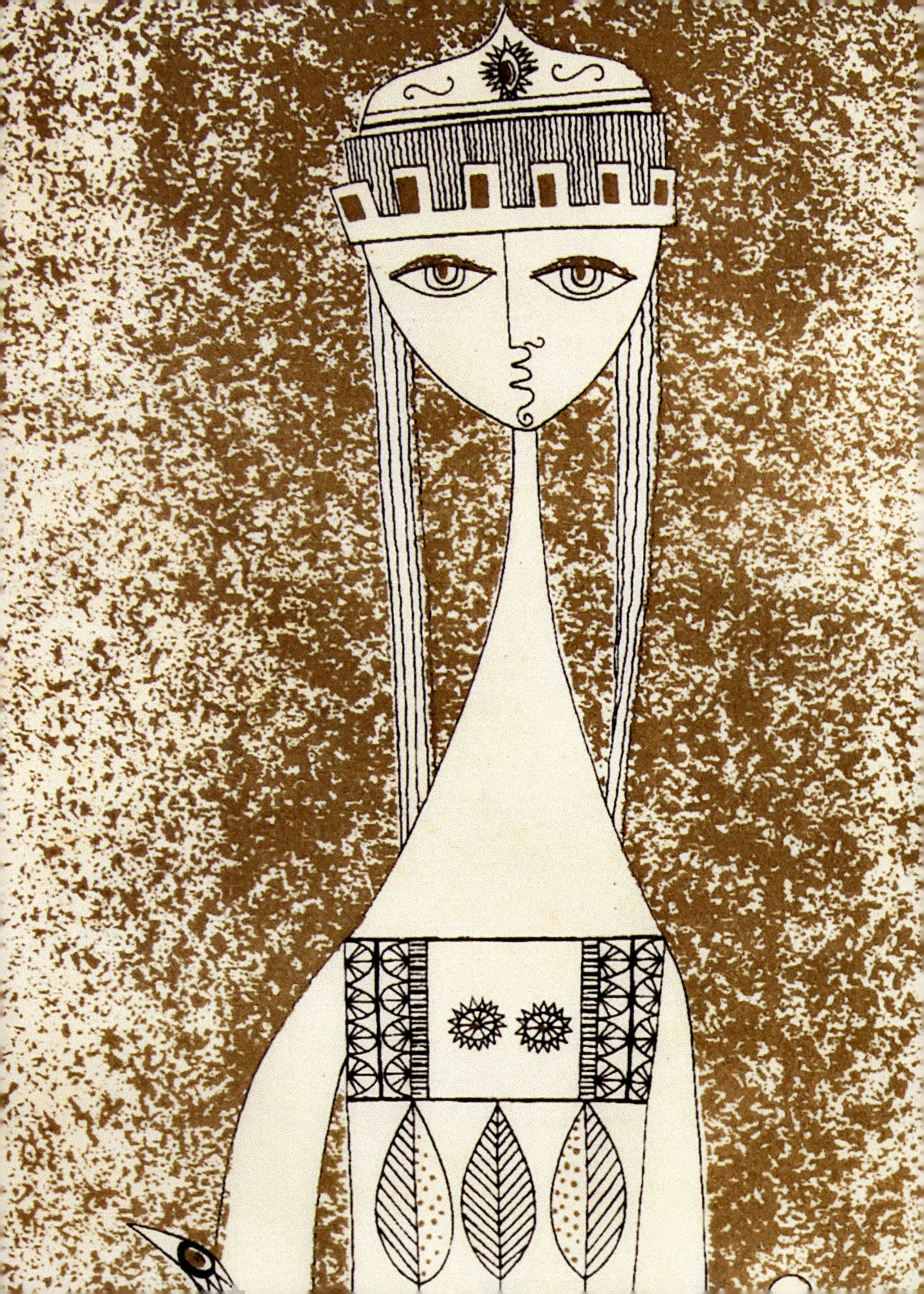

SILK SCREENS

DALE CAROLYN GLUCKMAN AND JO LAURIA

The Ackermans learned silk-screening techniques in the late 1940s. For their first apartment, while they were still living in Detroit, Jerome designed and made a silk screen to decorate plain cotton muslin. He asked his friend Ruben Eshkanian, a commercial textile artist who later worked at Knoll, to print the fabric so it could be made into drapes. At the same time, Evelyn hand silk screened a series of cards for her sister-in-law's business, Lucé Lipton Interior Design Studio. Ultimately, she created a joyful Christmas card using the printing method and licensed it to Signet in the mid-1950s.

Because the Ackermans had experience with the silk-screening process, they added products using that printing technique to their ERA product line early on as they continued to investigate new design avenues for wall decoration. They put a great deal of effort into researching materials and tried the technique on paper, linen, felt, burlap, and window shades—ultimately selecting linen and felt as the best surfaces for screenprinting. As with their other textiles, the designs were offered in warm and cool combinations. The Ackermans outsourced the silk screen production to a company in Los Angeles, where the process was still done by hand.

In a 1965 marketing letter, the Ackermans described the silk-screen process variously employed in their products: "This is basically a stencil process where the stencil materials are applied to silks of very fine mesh. The [ink] colors are hand-mixed to be a perfect match to the artist's specifications. These colors are then 'squeegeed,' also by hand, through the stencil onto the fabric. The silk-screen method has its own distinctive and original qualities. Because of its flexibility, it permits an unlimited range in the use of such design elements as line or solid, variations from delicacy to boldness, transparency, and opacity of color. The technique, therefore, offers opportunities for rich artistic manipulation."

This product line was relatively small, starting with five designs in 1958 that were priced lower than the woven and hooked textiles. Early designs evoke the elongated forms Evelyn had first used to decorate Jenev ceramics. All the silk screens were figural as compared to the woven tapestries and hooked wall hangings, which included geometric and abstract shapes. *Kites*, shown in *California Design IV* in 1958, depicts two young girls holding kites and is as much about the play of shape, pattern, and color as the figures themselves. It was executed in only four colors (and therefore only four screens)—blue, purple, orange, and tan—but more colors are created by printing one color over another. A sense of texture on a flat print is mimicked by stippling and the use of color areas that do not solidly fill shapes, giving a hand-drawn appearance.

As the ERA tapestry, hooking, and woodcarving lines increased and they imported wall hangings from Europe and Scandinavia, the sales of the silk screens diminished. They were ultimately dropped from the ERA product offerings in 1966. In 1973 however, they revitalized the technique to reinterpret two handwoven tapestry designs—*Morning Dove* and *Aerial View*—on linen in custom colors for the architect Charles Luckman for the Hyatt Regency Hotel in the Broadway Plaza, Los Angeles.

OPPOSITE Detail of *Girl with Bird*, a 1957 silk screen, reflects Evelyn's illustrative figural style. OVERLEAF LEFT The pair, *Girl with Lyre* and *Girl with Bird*, 10-by-44-inch silk screens, complement the attenuated female figures with a myriad of patterns on their sheath dresses. Evelyn often employed the theme of a woman holding an instrument, a bird, or flowers. The gold was an experimental color; the turquoise and navy colorway was also offered in orange and black. OVERLEAF RIGHT The cheeky *Acrobats* in their striped leotards, one atop the other, evoke the whimsical feel of Bjørn Wiinblad's work. Printed on felt, the figures are primarily turquoise in hue with a simple shift in ground colors. PAGES 202–203 Hand printed on tan burlap in a simple three-color palette of black, orange, and white, the 1958 *Jester*, *Hobby Horse*, and *Minstrel* silk screens, each measuring 18 by 48 inches, were a creative play on the patterned costumes of the harlequins. The *Jester* detail reveals an experiment on embossed Masonite that mimics the texture of burlap.

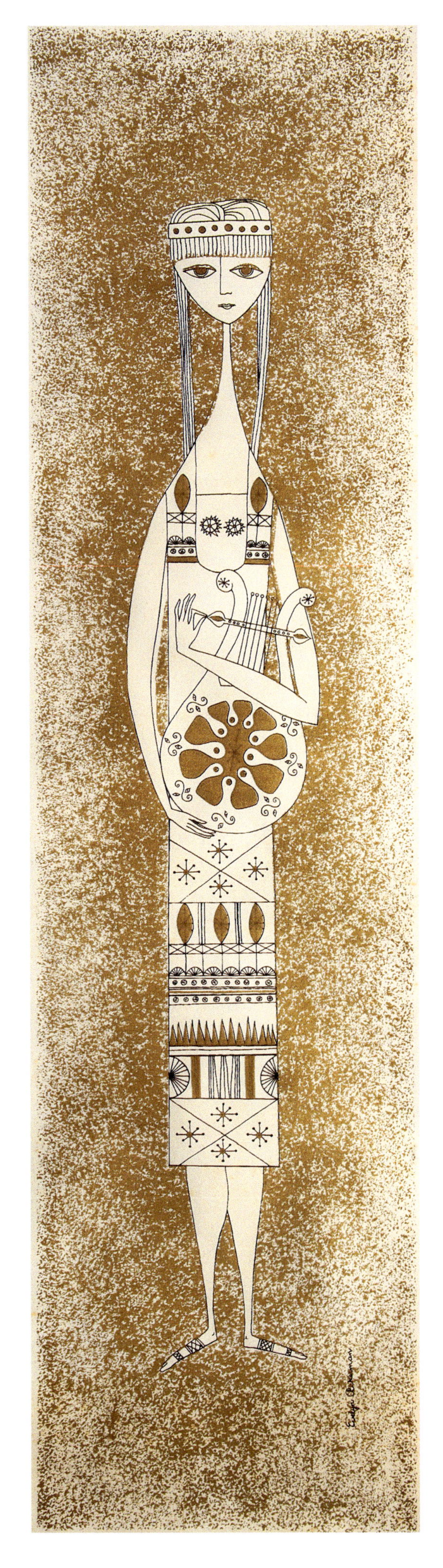

OPPOSITE Evelyn's ability to create complex yet complementary patterns in her designs is highlighted in her first silk screen in 1956. The 28-by-52-inch *Kites* selected for *California Design IV*, was hand printed in Los Angeles. The Ackermans experimented with felt, shown here, and window shade material but ultimately chose linen. ABOVE "A Signet Christmas card by Evelyn Ackerman," was silk screened by hand and available from the company with or without a name imprinted below the "Happy New Year" line on the interior. The 5-by-7-inch card combines angel, bird, tree, ornament, and star forms with decorative letters. At the bottom left, a candy cane and peppermint join the "Y" of "Merry" to spell "Joy."

EA

EA

EA

WOODCARVINGS

JO LAURIA AND DALE CAROLYN GLUCKMAN

In 1957 Evelyn designed and Jerry produced their first carved bas-reliefs. Included among these were *Saint George and the Dragon*, and a triptych of *Adam, Eve*, and *Garden*. As Jerry explored how to increase production and efficiency while maintaining quality, he turned to the multiple spindle-carving techniques of furniture manufacturing to replicate their hand-carved wood designs. Jerry approached a small Southern California furniture carver, Maurice Spinak. The Ackermans' designs were completely unrelated to the furniture components he carved, but Spinak was intrigued. As their market grew in the early 1960s, they looked to increase capacity and moved to a larger firm, A&M Woodcarving. Jerry focused on productivity while maintaining quality and reasonable price points. This led the Ackermans to standardize sizes, requiring Evelyn to design within the constraints of the material and dimensions.

The warmth and character of the wood designs complemented both traditional and contemporary interiors and were popular in furniture, department, and gift stores, mail-order catalogs, and, due to many animal motifs, even gift shops in zoos. The Ackermans visualized these bas-relief carvings in sculptural terms. Evelyn drew the design to size for the "pattern" or "master" and included detailed instructions indicating as many as five different carving depths to produce dimensional layers. She retained tool marks to create texture and surface interest, and softened radiuses to produce a "sculptural effect." To reduce costs, Evelyn often requested limitation to two tools. She encouraged Danny Moran, the master woodcarver at A&M, to use his judgment and address any machine-specific constraints. After a master was hand-carved, the Ackermans reviewed it at the shop. Once approved, the master was placed in the middle of a pantographlike machine with up to 24 vertical routers over blank stock. The carver would follow the master over the contours to rough out multiples of each design, and the mechanically carved pieces were then hand-finished to give a crafted look. Each piece was slightly different. Early designs were carved in walnut, but when this wood became too expensive, Jerry substituted ash, another hardwood, finished with a walnut stain and wax.

In 1963 the Ackermans' former business partner, Sherrill Broudy, approached them to produce carved panels leveraging the multiple-spindle method at A&M. Together they established the new enterprise, Panelcarve. From this project, the concept arose to develop modular, carved redwood panels with tongue-and-groove edge detail that could be easily assembled for architectural and interior design applications. Allowing maximum flexibility and customization by varying the combination of designs, the 9-by-36-inch and 9-by-84-inch panels were especially popular for doors and walls. The *900 Series*, like *Evie's Birds*, were single, large-scale slabs. Broudy asked Evelyn to create the first group of designs. The *Ucello* motifs of birds, flowers, plants, and stems became the core of the Panelcarve product line. In quick succession over two years, Evelyn created more than 25 designs for Panelcarve, including *Castles* and *Zodiac* designs. The line rapidly gained national attention and a year after its introduction, the May 1964 issue of *Arts & Architecture* noted Panelcarve "retains the best of the old while adapting it to the new." Although the Ackermans sold their interest in Panelcarve back to Broudy, Evelyn continued to design for the company and by 1969 had contributed nearly 50 products. The *Animal Woodblocks*, marketed by both ERA and Panelcarve, served as an example of modularity in carved wood panels from this period. ERA sold both individual blocks and Panelcarve pieces with multiple animals on each.

Panelcarve installations are still extant on residential and commercial buildings such as banks, restaurants, hotels, and universities, including the UCLA Faculty Center, Alan Ladd Building in Palm Springs, and the University of Kentucky.

Jerry initially took over the marketing of Panelcarve and featured the product line in their ERA showroom and promoted it nationwide. When Panelcarve broadened its offerings and became Forms+Surfaces, Jerry continued to sell through ERA. This marketing system—with Jerry representing the product line for both companies—formed the core of the relationship that continued for over 20 years.

In 1973 the Ackermans extended the ERA wood products by developing a line of popular giftware items, including gourmet accessories and plant holders, using a series of smaller plaques designed by Evelyn. Over the next few years, this group grew to include nearly 60 different designs. The gourmet line was generally carved in natural ash to fit in well with kitchens. Inspired by the growing market exemplified by Macy's Cellar, Jerry adapted the designs to different uses, including knife holders, spice racks, and napkin holders, all retailing for $30 or less. *Plant Huggers*, produced in redwood for its outdoor durability, were available in a selection of box, circular, and wrought iron holders.

Assuming their place alongside other successful ERA offerings of domestic decor and accessories, the carved wood bas-reliefs were varied, versatile, and affordable as either singular decorative elements or combined in panels where their modularity made them especially attractive to residential and commercial clients who required flexible design solutions. The spindle-carved wood bas-reliefs remained a staple in ERA's product line until the company's closure in the 1980s.

OPPOSITE *Adam*, *Eve*, and *Garden* were designed in 1958 as a slender triptych of 7-by-36-inch carvings. All three were exhibited in *California Design VII*. While the figures were discontinued in 1971, *Garden* was produced for another 10 years.

OPPOSITE The master carver Danny Moran holds *Evie's Birds* in a Panelcarve catalog printed soon after its 1966 debut. Offered in left and right orientations, the large redwood panel, measuring 21 by 63 inches, was intended to be attached to standard doors, but was often used in other ways. ABOVE LEFT The 1958 *Saint George and the Dragon*, the first wood piece in *California Design V*, shows Evelyn's ability to maximize a narrative in a woodcarving that measures 8 by 33 inches. The sinuous lines of the dragon contrast with the flattened portrayal of Saint George bracketed by a crenelated top and bottom evoking a medieval castle. ABOVE RIGHT In *Adam and Eve*, the first couple sits hand-in-hand under a tree. The 9-by-21-inch carving was designed in 1969.

ABOVE The drawing for *Flora de Madera* in cotton candy pinks may seem like an illustration, but in actuality the colors and shading designate the depth of the carving. The 9-by-24-inch size was intended for leftover pieces of ash. OPPOSITE The 1964 hand-carved master for *Flora de Madera* reflects Evelyn's instructions for the face and hands, a "simple sculptural effect with a certain amount of delicacy and sweetness of expression." The master was placed in the multiple spindle machine and followed by the carver to replicate the design. OVERLEAF Murray Feldman designed a number of executive desks clad in Panelcarve designs for Chairs Unlimited. The 1964 *Candelabra* was paired with a Jack Boyd sculpture in this *California Design IX* installation photograph.

PREVIOUS PAGES Included in *California Design XI*, the 1969 *Animal Woodblocks* consisted of 20 designs in 9½-inch squares and 9½-by-19-inch rectangles. The deeply carved redwood plaques were often pickled with an ageing agent. The breadth of influences created a fanciful menagerie that could be used individually or clustered together. The designs were also available as Panelcarve for architectural applications—designer to the stars Steve Chase used them on the front door of Sonny and Cher's home in Palm Springs, California. ABOVE *Ucello*, the first design for Panelcarve, became iconic and was on the cover of the new line's first catalog. The naturalistic designs of birds, flowers, plants, seeds, stems, and borders could be mixed and matched in 9-by-36-inch pieces to any scale for interior or exterior. OPPOSITE In November 1963, *Interior Previews West Coast Sourcebook* included the article "Evelyn & Jerome Ackerman: A Creative Combination in ERA" and featured *Ucello* panels on the cover. The next year at the 1964 World's Fair in New York, *Ucello* doors were displayed at the Pavilion of American Interiors.

NTERIOR PREVIEWS
EST COAST SOURCE BOOK / NOV.-DEC., 1963

FORMS + SURFACES

OPPOSITE A door to the Crystal Shores apartment building in Incline Village, Nevada, one of Sherrill Broudy's projects, featured the 1963 design *Castles* shown on the cover of a Forms+Surfaces catalog. The popular design was offered in 9-by-48-inch and 9-by-84-inch panels. The same Panelcarve design adorns the mid-century UCLA Faculty Center by Austin, Field & Fry and Welton Becket. ABOVE *Plant Huggers*, shown in a vintage catalog page, were available in 9-by-6-inch, and 9-by-12-inch sizes, in redwood and ash, stained and unstained, and could be used outdoors or indoors. Jerry's creative ability to conceptualize product design applications around Evelyn's pieces was reflective of their partnership.

METAL AND HYDRASTONE

JO LAURIA AND DALE CAROLYN GLUCKMAN

Jerry's willingness to experiment with new production methods and materials was one of the factors in their successful business development. Sand-cast aluminum, anodized aluminum, and chem milling (a chemical etching-removal technique for metal developed by the aerospace industry) exemplified his ability to apply industrial processes to design.

In 1955 Evelyn designed *Warrior King*, a cast aluminum bas-relief. The production process began by creating a full-sized clay model mounted to a board. They asked the metalworker who had been making frames for the mosaic panels and tables to sand cast the design in molten aluminum. Once cast, the pieces were often accented with mosaic tile inlay in the crown and breastplate. Following the introduction of the metal bas-reliefs in 1956, the Ackermans created several special metal commissions, including two projects for the architects Kanner & Mayer, a bird sculpture for Chandler's Shoes in Pasadena, California, and etched panels for a women's clothing store. Jerry's sculpture was made free form in aluminum while Evelyn's panels were chem-milled in gold anodized aluminum. In 1957 they briefly produced and sold an anodized aluminum *Four Seasons Perpetual Calendar.* While the Ackermans explored enamel on copper plates with Sascha Brastoff, a prominent ceramist whose showroom and studio were across the street from ERA, this collaboration did not result in a commercial venture.

In 1958 Jerry designed a porcelain-enameled steel candelabra in angled alternating color panels that was produced by a commercial enameling company in Southern California. The lustrous shades of orange and ochre, yellow and ecru, or cerulean and light blue resulted in a warm reflection of the candles, which were held in the brass-plated arms that extended from the enameled surface. Available as table and wall models, the modular shapes and coordinated colors could be used individually or combined to create a larger display. In a June 1, 1958 article, the *San Francisco Chronicle* exclaimed, "Most vivid of all is . . . zigs of sharp ochre yellow and zags of the most brilliant orange that human eyes can comfortably bear."

Soon, the Ackermans added hardware, which ultimately became a mainstay of ERA's product line. After meeting the designer Pepe Mendoza on a 1957 trip to Mexico, they introduced his brass and turquoise pieces—hardware, tables, lanterns—to the United States in 1958. In 1959 ERA imported Danish hardware, becoming the exclusive United States distributor of recessed plastic pulls by Danish Count Sigvard Bernadotte.

These trendsetting products were popular with architects, designers, and cabinetmakers—even boat manufacturers. Over time they added additional hardware lines from Barbizon (France), Citterio Giulio (Italy), and Sugatsune (Japan).

That same year, alongside the Bernadotte and Mendoza pieces, the Ackermans introduced their own line of hardware consisting of hand-cast solid-brass knobs and pulls produced in Florence, Italy. This required the coordination of multiple family-run firms specializing in different casting, inlay, and mosaic techniques. "There is nothing machine-like about these pulls except the threaded screw hole," proclaimed an ERA marketing letter. The hardware was not merely functional, it was decorative. The dramatic *Horse* and *King* and *Queen* pulls, with their large-scale and complex patterns, were offered in stylish inlays of lapis lazuli, turquoise, vermillion agate, and Granito Nero (black marble mixed with mother of pearl).

A dizzying variety of cabinet hardware, mostly designed by the Ackermans, and marble and onyx pieces by Sherrill Broudy, were made in jewel-colored micromosaics, marble and stone, and luminous copper enamel. The Ackermans also added to their contemporary designs traditional Italian mosaics, cameos, and marble pieces.

By 1965 Jerry created a new hardware line to fill a gap in the contemporary market. The result was the *Antico* group of hand-cast solid-brass hardware—14 different knobs and pulls that embodied "the look of antiquity . . . but new in design." Produced in various sizes, the designs reflected an organic, hand-hewn appearance cast in deep relief and were oxidized to achieve a soft green patina reminiscent of ancient bronze. Some of the pulls, knobs, and escutcheons were also available in polished metal with stone inlay, while others had mosaic inlay. Like the earlier *Horse* and *King* and *Queen* pulls, the hardware line was shown in the *California Design* exhibitions.

Evelyn's *Three Musicians* plaque, designed in 1955 and exhibited in *California Design II*, was first cast in cement. But the weight made it challenging, so the Ackermans explored a new material, Hydrastone, that could be cast like plaster but was lighter and lent itself to intricate detail. In 1964 they expanded the production of Hydrastone, and Evelyn designed a line of whimsical decorative bas-relief plaques, bookends, and sculptures that were hand-cast and hand-painted by artisans in Southern California.

OPPOSITE Evelyn adapted a favorite motif of a *King* and *Queen* to large-scale, 18-inch-high door handles that were cast in brass and inlaid with a variety of materials. The pair was featured in *California Design VIII* along with the *Horse* pulls.

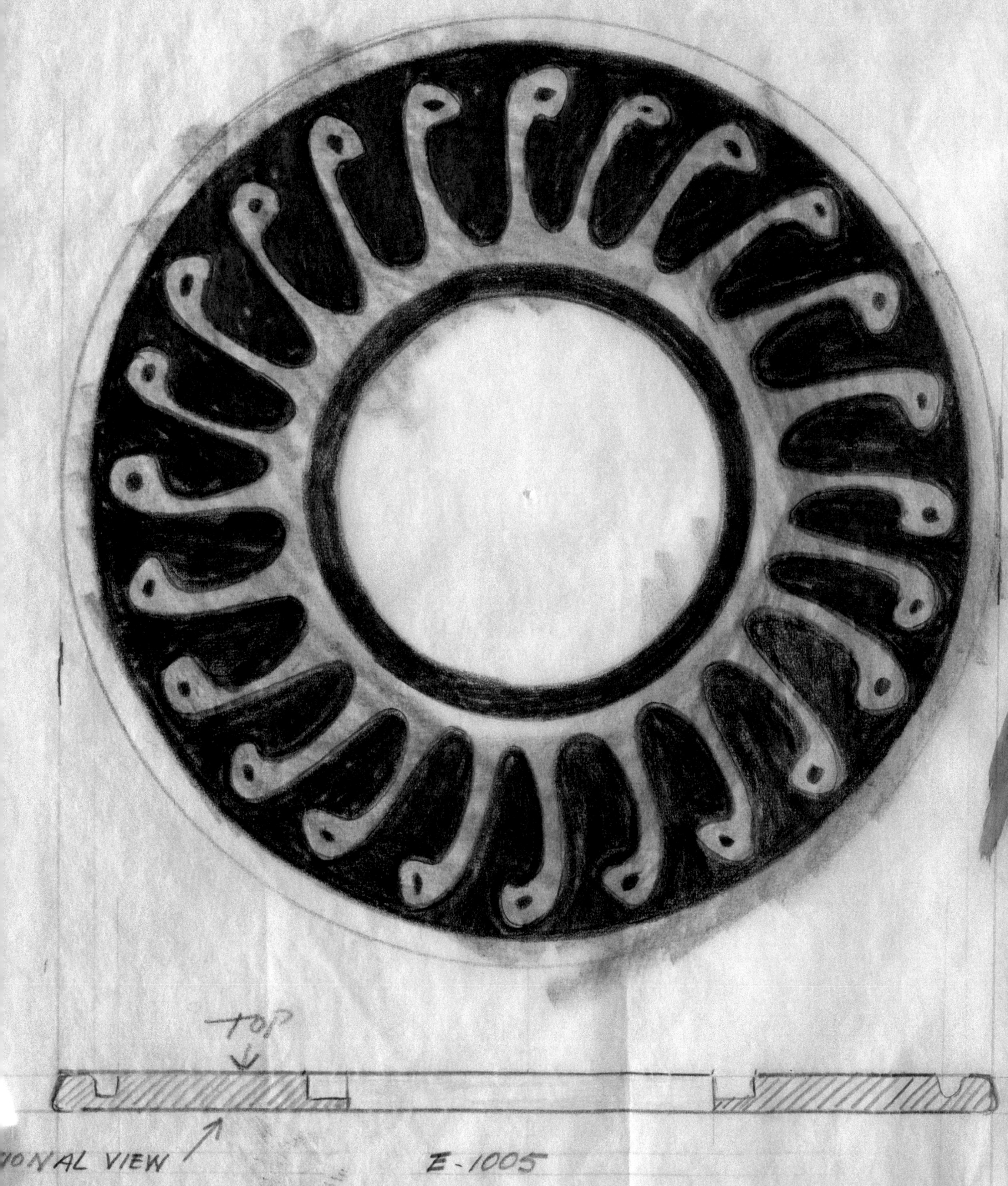
TOP
IONAL VIEW
E-1005

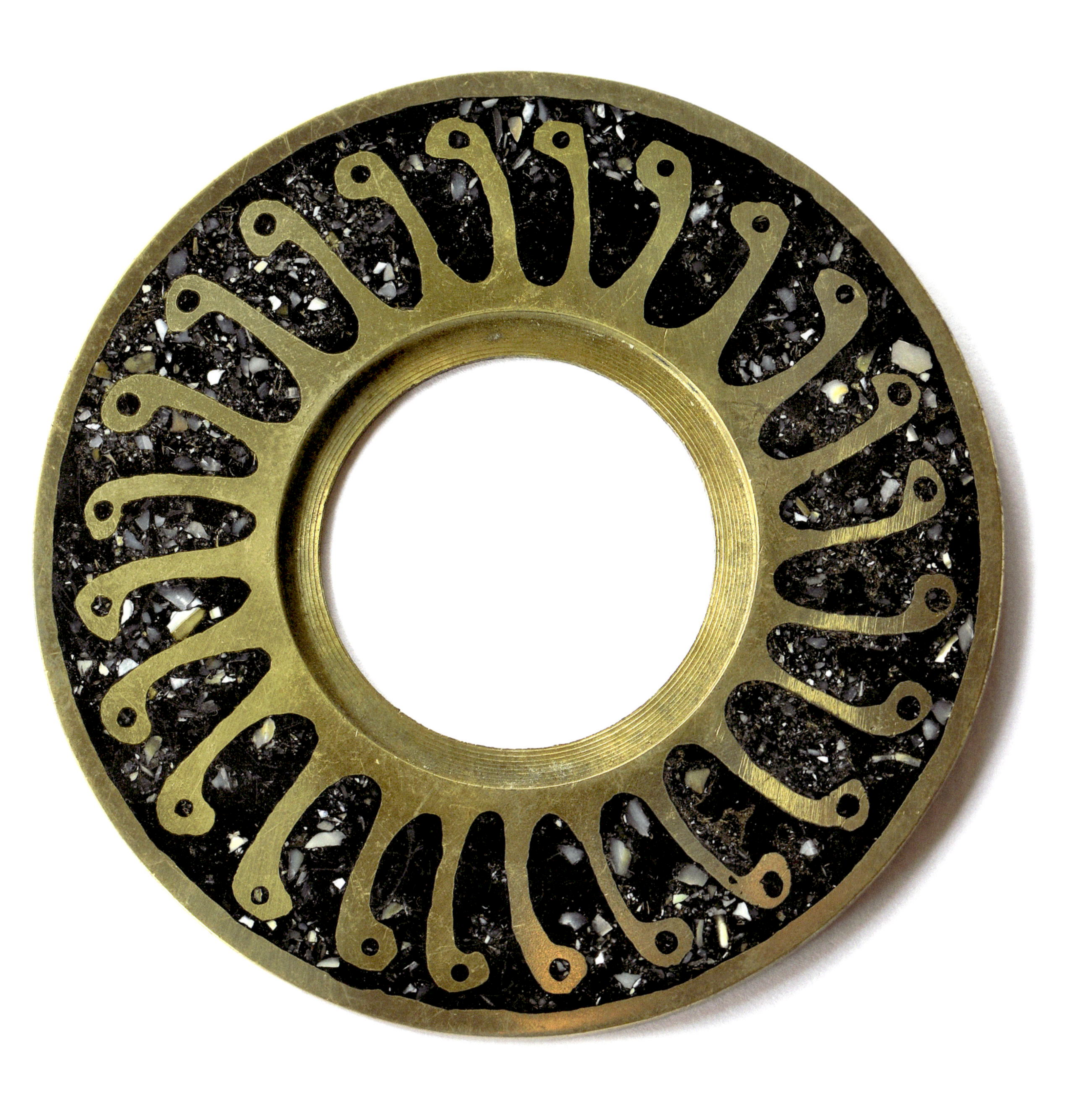

OPPOSITE The full-sized drawing for the inlaid escutcheon provided an elevation for the Italian manufacturer to hand cast the piece. ABOVE The solid-brass escutcheon was meant to go behind a doorknob. The black mother-of-pearl inlay created a sophisticated counterpoint to the brass tendrils. OVERLEAF This 1965 ERA catalog page shows the variety of sizes and shapes of *Antico* hardware. The pieces, included in *California Design IX*, could be easily mixed because of Jerry's organic lines, consistent scale, deep relief, and oxidized *verde* finish.

a new wide, wonderful world of

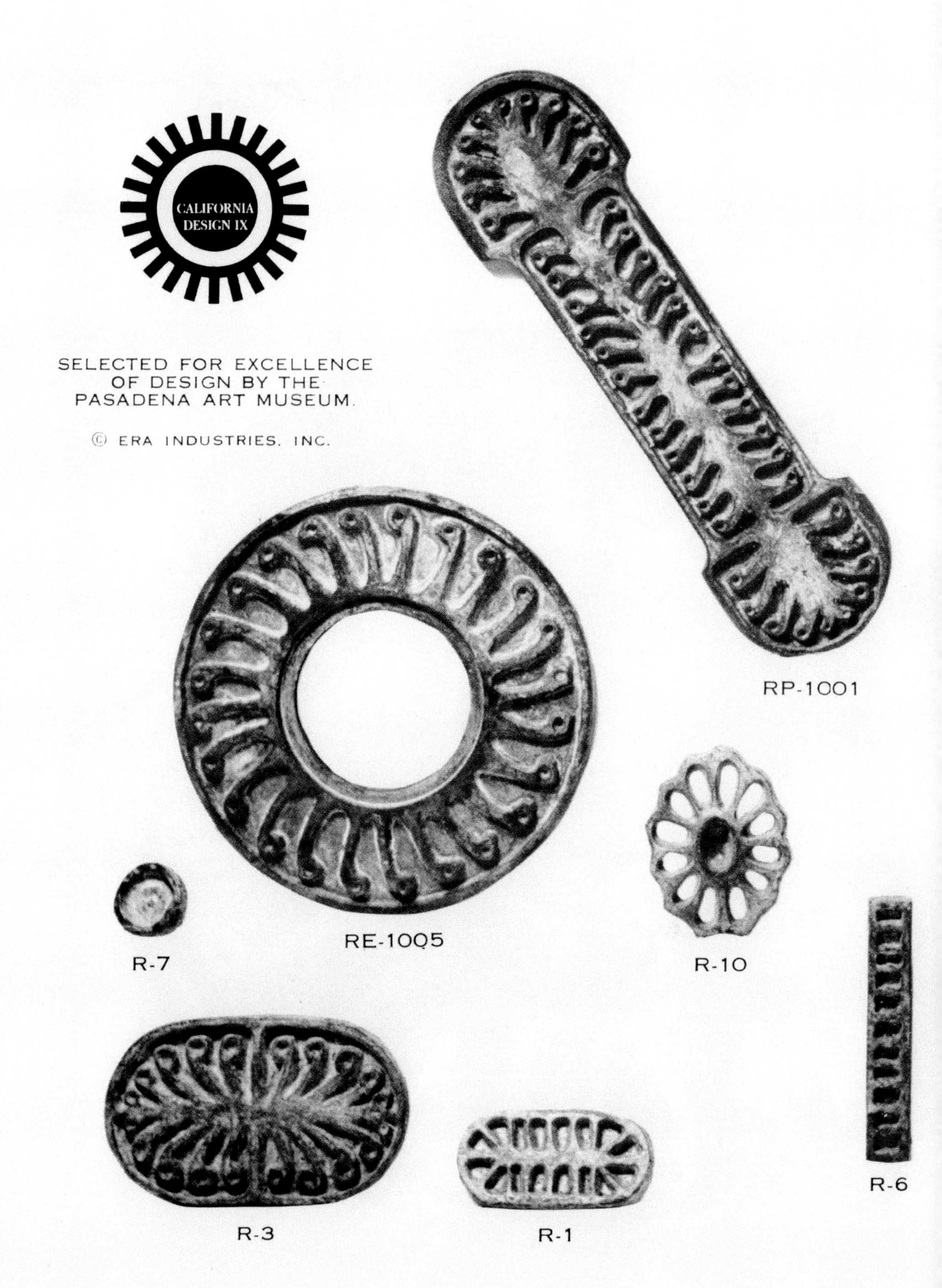

ERA INDUSTRIES, INC. • 8817 BEVERLY BOULEVARD • LOS ANGEL

HARDWARE

ANTICO

THE LOOK OF ANTIQUITY... BUT NEW IN DESIGN . . . ANTICO PULLS/KNOBS AND ESCUTCHEON PLATES . . . HAND CAST OF SOLID BRASS . . . WITH RICHLY CARVED DESIGNS IN DEEP RELIEF . . . OXIDIZED TO ACHIEVE THE SOFTLY GLOWING MULTI-HUED GREEN PATINA OF ANCIENT BRONZE. DESIGNED BY JEROME ACKERMAN. HANDCRAFTED IN ITALY.

R-4

R-8

RE-1006

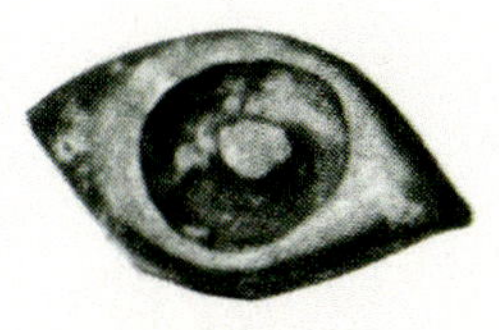

RP-1000 R-5 R-9 R-2

ERA

FORNIA 90048

OPPOSITE *Antico* pulls, each 8¼ inches high, reveal the brass under the verdigris patina after 40 years of use in the Ackerman kitchen. The only machine-made feature of the hardware was the threaded screw hole. ABOVE Jerry experimented with inlays in some of the 1965 *Antico* pieces. In this 3⅝-inch pull, polished brass sets off the turquoise inlay. The Ackermans were always thinking about what they could do that would be different and trend forward. OVERLEAF The curvaceous shape of the 1959 *Horse* door pull, combined with its rich vermillion agate inlay and pattern, transformed a functional piece of hardware into a dramatic work of art. When used in mirror-image pairs, the pulls, each 6½ by 10 inches, made a strong statement on doors and cabinetry.

PREVIOUS PAGES The Ackermans compared hardware to jewelry for cabinets. These brass beauties, part of the ERA "MP" series launched in the late 1950s, came in a variety of shapes, sizes, and inlays. OPPOSITE The original clay model and mold for casting *Warrior King* in molten aluminum. ABOVE Brandishing a sword overhead, the 25-by-26-inch *Warrior King* bas-relief, shown in *California Design III*, evoked a Picasso-esque quality. The sand-cast aluminum enhanced the details of the chain mail, beard, and shield in Evelyn's 1957 design. The crown and breastplate were often inlaid with mosaic tile.

OPPOSITE The winsome 1958 12-by-36-inch *Adolescent* bas-relief was available both in sand-cast aluminum and as a cast plaque. The design flows along an S-curve from the young woman's ponytail to her wind-blown skirt. ABOVE The Los Angeles-based architectural firm Kanner & Mayer worked with the Ackermans on custom contract jobs. In 1956 Jerry designed a metal sculpture for Robert Mayer for Chandler's shoe store in Pasadena, California, shown in a Julius Shulman photograph. The branches were drawn free-form, then sand cast, later assembled, and the bird and flower forms added at the end.

PREVIOUS PAGES In 1958 Jerry designed porcelain-enameled steel candelabra in alternating color panels. The tabletop and wall models all held glass votives. OPPOSITE Designed in 1955 the *Three Musicians* plaque referenced classical figures in togas with a modern flair. The 12-by-24-inch plaque was shown in *California Design II* in 1956. ABOVE The hand-painted whimsical *Berry Hunt* demonstrates Evelyn's ability to illustrate with what the contemporary designer Jonathan Adler referred to as "a childlike sense of wonder."

A RETURN TO STUDIO CRAFT

JEFFREY HEAD

By the mid-1980s, Evelyn and Jerry decided to stop designing and manufacturing new products for ERA and instead focus their creative energies on individual projects. Evelyn, a highly respected collector of antique dolls and toys, devoted time to reseach and writing on the subject. After a nearly 30-year hiatus from working in ceramics to run ERA, Jerry returned to the studio in 1990 to create hand-thrown and slab-constructed ceramics. He retrieved his original Jenev molds and cast pieces in them until just before his 99th birthday.

While still a traditional potter by training and perspective—he admired Shoji Hamada, Bernard Leach, and John Foster—Jerry explored new surface treatments, particularly geometric carving, and introduced more figural and whimsical decoration. His contemporary work ranged from functional vessels to sculptural forms in cone 10-reduction-fired stoneware. The vigorous forms, decorative features, and glazing show his mature, innate command as a ceramist, and the work has been exhibited in galleries and museums and is held in the collections of the Los Angeles County Museum of Art and the Renwick Gallery of the Smithsonian American Art Museum. One-man and group shows followed, echoing participation in similar events 50 years earlier.

While Jerry continued to represent several lines to architects and designers and participate in ceramic sales, Evelyn served as a founding member of the Culver City Arts Committee in 1988. The group was responsible for the selection and placement of public art in the city.

The masterwork from this period was Evelyn's *Stories from the Bible* cloisonné series, completed in 1985. Evelyn worked on the series every day for a year and a half, considering it her most challenging and gratifying creation and the most important expression of herself. Each cloisonné represented her interpretation of 40 stories from the Bible, including, among others, Adam and Eve, Cain and Abel, Jonah and the Whale, and Jacob's Ladder. The complicated, multistep technique required intense concentration using a magnifying lamp and truly became a labor of love. *Stories from the Bible* resides in the Renwick Gallery in Washington, D.C.

To create the series, Evelyn started with a 3⅛-inch square copper tile, glazed the front and back with a clear enamel, and fired it to prevent warping. She then bent the silver wire (cloisons), following her drawing. The wire was glued in place, and the tile was fired to stabilize the wire and sink it into the top of the tile glaze to keep it in place. Evelyn filled in the spaces separated by the silver with translucent colored-powder enamels using a watercolor brush—a painstaking, tedious process that enabled her to achieve a graceful level of detail. Once the enamel powders were in place, she fired the cloisonné, and the powder liquefied, spread, and hardened. All the colored powders were fired at once and essentially became glass. There was some shrinkage from the firing so the entire surface was rubbed by hand with a special stone before it was filled and fired again. The smoothing also gave the tile a glossy finish. Firing time for each step was less than a minute, compared to firing clay, which, depending on a variety of factors, can take up to 11 hours.

The ceramics and cloisonnés, as with all the Ackermans' commercial and studio pieces, showed a commitment to making beautiful objects. It was also a way for the couple to share their own values and aesthetic: their experience of modernism through the very objects they made for others.

Forty "design legends" gathered in 1994 for *A Secret History of Design in Los Angeles* at the Pacific Design Center, site of the Ackermans' last showroom. Many of the designers were peers Jerry and Evelyn had known for decades. The group included Cleo Baldon, Don Chadwick, Elsie Crawford, Arthur Ellsworth, John Follis, Miller Fong, Gere Kavanaugh, Max and Rita Lawrence, Mary Jane Leland, John and Marilyn Neuhart, and Deborah Sussman.

Jerry and Evelyn's contributions to the decorative arts in Southern California, which began in the mid-20th century, came full circle in 2009, exactly 60 years after the exhibition *For Modern Living*, at the Detroit Institute of Arts, so pivotal in their development as designer-craftspersons. To inspire appreciation of their work for a new generation, Dale Carolyn Gluckman and Jo Lauria curated *Masters of California Mid-Century Modernism*, the first retrospective of the Ackermans' life as a design couple at the Mingei International Museum in San Diego. Since then, museums have continued to acquire their work and Jerry and Evelyn enjoyed other exhibitions from Los Angeles to New York and awards, including Distinguished Alumni awards from Wayne State University and Alfred University and the Los Angeles Conservancy Modern Masters Award.

Throughout their long design career, Evelyn and Jerry Ackerman remained creative spirits who pursued their interests together, yet maintained their individuality. Jerry reflected, "Our faith in ourselves and in each other created the foundation for our design partnership." Their love for each other remained unchanged during 64 years of marriage. Even in their later years, Evelyn remarked how her life would not have been possible without Jerry. And Jerry, who had always felt he was the lucky one, remained amazed at Evelyn's artistry.

OPPOSITE Each of Evelyn's 40 individual 3⅛-inch cloisonné squares in *Stories from the Bible* encapsulates a different story in a miniature composition.

ABOVE The brilliant jewel tones of the 1968 *Royal Rider* cloisonné were achieved by painstakingly layering and firing numerous translucent-glass color fills to create a smooth, polished surface. OPPOSITE Evelyn layered gold foil underneath the enamel of the *King and Queen*, also made in 1968, adding shimmer to the surface. The highly stylized figures are reminiscent of chess pieces.

ABOVE The Renwick Gallery of the Smithsonian American Art Museum in Washington, D.C. added the 1993 *Monks* to its craft collection. Persimmon-glazed figures form columns as legs for the crenelated bowl. OPPOSITE In 2004 at the age of 84, Jerry began a series of matte-black stoneware bowls in different shapes and decorated with applied fanciful figures. *See No Evil* combines four sitting figures and floral motifs with inscribed patterns. OVERLEAF A collection

of ceramics from 1990 to 2007 sits atop a 19th-century Japanese *tansu* chest in the Ackermans' living room. Jerry played with reptilian forms of alligators, frogs, snakes, and lizards and used a variety of decorative surface treatments—yet the glaze colors and patterns unify the work.

SELECTED BIBLIOGRAPHY

"100 Ways to Beautify Your Home: The Best of the *Los Angeles Times Home* Magazine." *Los Angeles Times*, 1961.

"Accessories: Design Within Reach." *Interior Design Market Tabloid*, May 18, 2018.

"Accessories That Reflect Personality." *Baltimore Sunday Sun* magazine, May 10, 1959.

Ackerman, Jerome, Laura Ackerman-Shaw, and Dan Chavkin. "Hand-in-Hand: The Designs of Evelyn and Jerome Ackerman." Panel, University Art Museum, California State University Long Beach, March 15, 2017.

Ackerman-Shaw, Laura. "Clay Culture: Jenev Re-release." *Ceramics Monthly*, Spring 2018.

Ackerman-Shaw, Laura. "Designs That Express Timeless Appeal." *Expressions*, 2017–18.

Ackerman-Shaw, Laura. "Evelyn and Jerome Ackerman: The House That Love Built." *Docomomo US Newsletter*, August 16, 2018.

Ackerman-Shaw, Laura. "In Tandem: The Life and Work of Jerry and Evelyn Ackerman." Presentation, Phoenix Modern Week, March 19, 2019.

Adler, Jonathan. "100 Ways to Happy Chic Your Life." *Sterling Signature*, 2012.

Anderson, Judith. "The Look Is Contemporary." *San Francisco Chronicle*, July 27, 1971.

Anderton, Frances. "Jerome and Evelyn Ackerman Revisited." Interview, *Design and Architecture on KCRW.com*, July 15, 2009.

Anderton, Frances. "The Ackermans: A Designing Couple." *Design and Architecture on KCRW.com*, February 15, 2011.

"An Exhibition of California Design." *Los Angeles Times Home* magazine, January 22, 1956.

"An Important New Correlation." *Los Angeles Times*, March 3, 1957.

"Arts of Daily Living." *House Beautiful*, October 1954.

Asay, Amber, and Laura Ackerman-Shaw. "Evelyn Ackerman." *Women Designers You Should Know* Podcast, episode 2, May 3, 2024.

Bailey, Catherine, Dale Carolyn Gluckman, Dave Hampton, Jo Lauria, Gerard O'Brien, Robin Petravic, and Keith York. "Perspectives on Mid-century California Design." Panel, Mingei International Museum, San Diego, June 27, 2009.

Barron, Stephanie, Sheri Bernstein, and Ilene Susan Fort. *Made in California: Art, Image, and Identity, 1900–2000*. Los Angeles: Los Angeles County Museum of Art; Berkeley: University of California Press, 2000.

Bartlett, Maxine. "Good Design." *Los Angeles Times Home* magazine, January 4, 1959.

Biondo, Adriene. "CB2 Line Honors Ackermans." *Eichler Network*, September 14, 2023.

Blauvelt, Andrew Satake, and Bartal Bridget, eds. *Eventually Everything Connects: Mid-Century Modern Design in the US*. New York: Phaidon, 2025.

Boone, Lisa. "Holiday Gift Guide 2014: 11 Books for Design Lovers." *Los Angeles Times*, December 4, 2014.

Bridges, Scott. "Culver City Artists Celebrated with Museum Exhibit." *Culver City News*, January 27, 2011.

California Design I. Pasadena: Pasadena Art Museum, 1955.

California Design II. Pasadena: Pasadena Art Museum, 1956.

California Design III. Pasadena: Pasadena Art Museum, 1957.

"California Design III—Pasadena Art Museum." *Arts & Architecture*, April 1957.

California Design IV. Pasadena: Pasadena Art Museum, 1958.

California Design V. Pasadena: Pasadena Art Museum, 1959.

California Design VI. Pasadena: Pasadena Art Museum, 1960.

California Design VII. Pasadena: Pasadena Art Museum, 1961.

California Design VIII. Pasadena: Pasadena Art Museum, 1962.

California Design IX. Pasadena: Pasadena Art Museum, 1965.

California Design X. Pasadena: Pasadena Art Museum, 1968.

California Design XI. Pasadena: Pasadena Art Museum, 1971.

California Design '76. Los Angeles: Pacific Design Center, 1976.

"California Designed, an Exhibition." *Arts & Architecture*, July 1955.

"California Designers Present." *Living for Young Homemakers*, December 1955.

"Carvings—by Man and by Machine." *Los Angeles Times Home* magazine, January 24, 1965.

Castellucci, Mike. "Good Morning San Diego." Broadcast, KUSI, San Diego, March 30, 2009.

Celeste, Sophia. "Exclusive: CB2 Launches the Ackerman Modern Collection." *Women's Wear Daily*, August 24, 2023.

Chavkin, Dan, Jeffrey Head, and Jo Lauria. *Architectural Pottery: Ceramics for a Modern Landscape*. New York: Monacelli, 2024.

Chavkin, Dan, and Lisa Thackaberry. *Hand-in-Hand: Ceramics, Mosaics, Tapestries, and Woodcarvings by the California Mid-century Designers Evelyn and Jerome Ackerman*. New York: Pointed Leaf Press, 2014.

Chessler, Suzanne. "Motown Modernists." *Detroit Jewish News*, April 13, 2006.

Chipman, Jack. *California Pottery Scrapbook: Identification and Value Guide*. Paducah, KY: Collector Books, 2005.

Clyde, Patricia. "Folklore in Carving." *Grand Rapids Press*, March 22, 1980.

Cusack, Anne. "A Peek Inside the Home of Crafts Masters Jerome and Evelyn Ackerman." Slideshow, *LATimes.com*, Home section, March 2009.

Daniels, Hope. "Renwick Celebrates 25." *American Style*, Summer 1997.

"Decorative Designs in Redwood." *Arts & Architecture*, May 1964.

DePuydt, Elise. *A Photo Guide to Fountains and Sculptures of Ojai: Art, History, and Architecture*. Oak View, CA: Sun Coast Enterprises, 2009.

DePuydt, Elise. "Meditation Mount Modernists Rediscovered." *Ojai Quarterly*, Summer 2011.

"Design in California and Mexico, 1915–1985." *American Art Review*, February 2018.

Edwards, Nadine M. "Let's Go to the Circus." *Los Angeles Times Home* magazine, December 14, 1970.

Elliott, David. "Make Mine Mingei." *San Diego News Network*, May 23, 2009.

Elliot-Bishop, James, Christy Johnson, Jo Lauria, Elaine Levin, Harold Nelson, Billie Sessions, and Cécile Whiting. *Common Ground: Ceramics in Southern California, 1945–1975*. Pomona, CA: American Museum of Ceramic Art, 2011.

Emanueli, Sharon K., Jo Lauria, and Eudorah M. Moore. *Golden State of Craft: California, 1960–1985*. Los Angeles: Craft and Folk Art Museum; Craft in America, 2011.

"ERA Industries." *Home Furnishings Daily*, October 9, 1967.

Feinstein Forman, Gail. "Jerome and Evelyn Ackerman's Shared Visions at Mingei." *San Diego Jewish World*, April 19, 2009.

"Finger Puppets: A Joy to Create, Child's Play to Animate." *House & Garden*, October 1966.

Friedman, Jane. "New Direction for American Craft." *Washington Post*, March 13, 1997.

Germany, Lisa, and Harry Gesner. *Houses of the Sundown Sea: The Architectural Vision of Harry Gesner*. New York: Abrams, 2012.

"Give Her the Gift of Handcrafts." *Los Angeles Times Home* magazine, June, 28, 1959.

Gluckman, Dale Carolyn, David Keeps, Gerard O'Brien, and Trina Turk. "Partners in Design: Evelyn and Jerome Ackerman." Panel, Palm Springs Modernism Week, February 20, 2020.

Gluckman, Dale Carolyn, and Jo Lauria. "A Marriage of Craft and Design: The Work of Evelyn and Jerome Ackerman." Curator's talk, Craft and Folk Art Museum, Los Angeles, March 27, 2011.

Gluckman, Dale Carolyn, and Jo Lauria. "Masters of Mid-century California Modernism: Evelyn and Jerome Ackerman." NPR interview, KPBS, March 26, 2009.

Griffin, Nancy. "Tip of the Week: Angled Candleholders." *San Francisco Chronicle*, June 1, 1958.

Guagliardo, Marco. "A Journey Through Love, Passion, Art, and Mid-Century Design," Interview, *Mid-Century Home*, November 13, 2024.

Hakanson, Joy. "Artists Pool Names, Talents in California Pottery Venture." *Detroit News*, April 12, 1955.

Halkin, Margaret, and Katie Nartonis. *In Tandem: The Life and Work of Jerry and Evelyn Ackerman*. Short film, 2015.

"Hardware with Spirit." *Los Angeles Examiner Pictorial Living*, December 11, 1960.

Harris, Jean. "Mosaics and Tapestries to Hang on Your Walls." *Detroit News*, November 19, 1957.

Head, Jeffrey. "Design Duo: Jerome and Evelyn Ackerman." *Modernism*, Spring 2005.

Head, Jeffrey. "Partners in Life and Design: Evelyn and Jerome Ackerman." Lecture, Mingei International Museum, San Diego, April 4, 2009.

Higby, Wayne. "The Ackerman Internship." *Ceramophile*, Fall 2022.

Hirst, Arlene. "A Designing Twosome Gets Its Due." *New York Times*, October 2, 2014.

Hodge, Brooke. "Seeing Things: Marriage by Design." *New York Times*, January 20, 2011.

Holm, Grace. "Evelyn Ackerman Design Shown." *Oregonian*, April 7, 1959.

Houseman, Robert E. "Brightest Little House in the West." *American Home, California Edition*, September 1963.

Hummon, David M. *Envisioning Jacob's Ladder: Religion, Representation, and Allusion in American Visual Culture, 1750–2000*. Worcester, MA: Iris and B. Gerald Cantor Gallery, College of the Holy Cross, 2004.

"Icons Remembered: Jerome Ackerman." *Ceramics Arts Yearbook*, 2020.

"Jerome Ackerman, Alfred University Alumnus, Leader in Modernist Decorative Art, Passes Away." Press release, Alfred University, May 3, 2019.

Johnson, Beverly E. "California Design, 1960." *Los Angeles Times Home* magazine, January 10, 1960.

Johnson, Beverly E. "California Design/9." *Los Angeles Times Home* magazine, March 28, 1965.

Kaplan, Wendy, ed. *California Design, 1930–1965: Living in a Modern Way*.

Los Angeles: Los Angeles County Museum of Art; Cambridge, MA: MIT Press, 2011.
Kaplan, Wendy, ed. *Found in Translation: Design in California and Mexico, 1915–1985*. Los Angeles: Los Angeles County Museum of Art; Munich: DelMonico Books/Prestel, 2017.
Kavanaugh, Gere. "A Secret History of Design in Los Angeles." *International Design Magazine*, March–April 1994.
Keeps, David A. "A Flair for the Whimsical." *Los Angeles Times*, Home section, March 28, 2009.
Keeps, David A. *"Palm Springs Eternal." Introspective Magazine*, November 29, 2017.
Keeps, David A. "Remembering Evelyn Ackerman, a Midcentury Master of Craft." *Los Angeles Times*, December 4, 2012.
Keeps, David A. "The Off Duty Holiday Gift Guide—50 Rare Finds: Collectible Candleholders, Reissued." *Wall Street Journal*, February 9, 2015.
Khazan, Olga. "Evelyn and Jerome Ackerman Design Their Own Love Story." *Design and Architecture on KCRW.com*, February 9, 2011.
Kohatsu, Gary. "Jerome Ackerman: A Life of Love, a Legacy by Design." *Culver City News*, May 2, 2019.
Krec, Ellen. "Beauty in Miniature." *Southland Sunday* magazine, November 15, 1970.
Krec, Ellen. "Don't Knock It, Pull It." *Long Beach Independent Press-Telegram Southland Magazine*, August 4, 1968.
Krec, Ellen. "They Carve Your Niche." *Long Beach Independent Press-Telegram Southland Magazine*, June 23, 1968.
Lauria, Jo. *Color and Fire: Defining Moments in Studio Ceramics, 1950–2000*. Los Angeles: Los Angeles County Museum of Art; New York: Rizzoli International, 2000.
Lauria, Jo. "Timeline: California's New Crafts Movement." *Archives of American Art Journal*, Fall 2011.
Lauria, Jo, and Suzanne Baizerman. *California Design: The Legacy of West Coast Craft and Style*. San Francisco: Chronicle Books, 2005.
Lauria, Jo, and Dale Carolyn Gluckman. "An Affair of the Heart." *Modern*, Summer 2012.
"Leadership Came West." *Los Angeles Times Home* magazine, July 15, 1956.
"Local Artist to Exhibit Work at Smithsonian." *Culver City News*, October 17, 1996.
Lopez, Rody. *Living with Clay: California Ceramics Collections*. Fullerton: California State University, 2020.
Lovelace, Joyce. "Basking in the 'Golden State of Craft.'" *American Craft Council*, October 5, 2011.
Lovelace, Joyce. "California Dreamers." Blog, *American Craft Magazine*, April 2009.
Lovelace, Joyce. "Mid-century Modernists." *American Craft Magazine*, June–July 2009.
Martin, Hannah. "Preview: Ceramics, Mosaics, Tapestries, and Wood Carvings by Jerome and Evelyn Ackerman." *Architectural Digest*, November 17, 2014.
Millier, Arthur. "Some of the Faces behind California Design." *Los Angeles Times Home* magazine, January 2, 1958.
"Mosaics." *San Francisco Examiner*, June 9, 1957.
"Mosaics: Bits of Beauty in Color." *Los Angeles Times Home* magazine, January 24, 1965.
"Mosaics: You Can Get Panels That Are Readymade." *San Francisco Examiner*, June 9, 1957.
Muchnic, Suzanne. "Jerome Ackerman, Who Stood at the Heart of L.A.'s Midcentury Modernism Movement, Dies at 99." *Los Angeles Times*, May 9, 2019.
Muto, Aya. "Evelyn and Jerry." *Kurashi No Techo* (Lifestyle) magazine, Summer 2011.
Nichols, Chris. "The Bright and Playful World of Ackerman Modern." *Los Angeles Magazine*, December 23, 2014.
Ohtake, Miyoko. "A Marriage of Craft and Design." *Dwell*, January 10, 2011.
Oliver, Steve. "Jerome and Evelyn Ackerman: California Crafts." Slideshow, *LATimes.com*, Home section, March 2009.
"On Exhibit California's Bright New Designs." *Los Angeles Times Home* magazine, January 12, 1958.
Peabody, Rebecca, Andrew Perchuk, Glenn Phillips, and Rani Singh, with Lucy Bradnock, eds. *Pacific Standard Time: Los Angeles Art, 1945–1980*. Los Angeles: Getty Research Institute; J. Paul Getty Museum, 2011.
Phillips, Kimberly. "Legends in Design: Evelyn and Jerome Ackerman." *Docomomo US Newsletter*, December 6, 2023.
Price, Steven. *Trousdale Estates: Midcentury to Modern in Beverly Hills*. New York: Regan Arts, 2017.
Rich, R. Michael. "The Faculty Club's Ackerman Panel Wall: A Fortuitous Discovery." *UCLA Faculty Club News*, April 2022.
Romas, David, ed. "Evelyn and Jerome Ackerman Celebrate 50 Years Leading an Art Movement." *Wayne State University CFPCA Expressions Newsletter*, Spring 2010.
"Showtime: Eighth National Decorative Arts-Ceramics Exhibition." *Ceramics Monthly*, July 1953.
Smart, George. "Interior Modernism 2: Sarah Archer and Laura Ackerman-Shaw." Interview, *US Modernist Radio*, no. 157, August 17, 2020.
Smithsonian Year. Washington, D.C.: Smithsonian Institution Press, 1997.
Soldner, Paul. "California Design/9." *Craft Horizons*, May–June 1965.
Steele, Victoria. "Ackerman Panels Restored." *UCLA Faculty Club News*, March 2022.
Stein, Lynne. *Hook, Prod, Punch, Tuft: Creative Techniques with Fabric and Fibre*. London: Herbert Press, Bloomsbury, 2023.
Steinberger, Staci. "Simpatico Modernism." *Modern Magazine*, Spring 2018.
Stern, Bill. *California's Designing Women, 1896–1986*. Los Angeles: Museum of California Design, 2013.
Stern, Bill and Peter Brenner. *California Pottery: From Missions to Modernism*. San Francisco: Chronicle Books, 2001.
Stevens, Kimberly. "Ackermans' Midcentury Style Back in Demand with Book, Film, Events." *Los Angeles Times*, February 7, 2015.
Stevens, Kimberly. "A Love Story in Modern Style." *Los Angeles Times*, February 7, 2015.
Stevens, Kimberly. "A Modernist Love Story." *Introspective Magazine*, June 1, 2015.
Stewart, Virginia. "Western Potters and Their Work." *Los Angeles Times Home* magazine, March 6, 1955.
"Talent That Has Few Boundaries." *Los Angeles Times Home* magazine, April, 23, 1961.
"Tapestries and Mosaics by Evelyn and Jerome Ackerman." *Arts & Architecture*, May 1961.
Thackaberry, Lisa. "Evelyn and Jerome Ackerman." Presentation, *Unsung Heroes of the American West #9 Passion Projects*, Society of Publication Designers, April 10, 2014.
"The Ackermans' Work Continues to Inspire New Generations of Art Enthusiasts." *Wayne State University CFPCA Newsletter*, 2019.
"The Work Never Gets Old for This Alfred University Alumnus." *Alfred University Newsletter*, January 5, 2018.
Tigerman, Bobbye. *A Handbook of California Design, 1930–1965: Craftspeople, Designers, Manufacturers*. Los Angeles: Los Angeles County Museum of Art; Cambridge, MA: MIT Press, 2013.
Tran, Vy. "The Iconic Stahl House Gets a Dreamy Makeover from Design Within Reach." *Design Milk*, March 12, 2018.
Trapp, Kenneth R., and Howard Risatti. *Skilled Work: American Craft in the Renwick Gallery*. Washington, D.C.: Smithsonian Institution Press, 1998.
Trounson, Rebecca. "Evelyn Ackerman Dies at 88; California Modernism Artist, Designer." *Los Angeles Times*, December 1, 2012.
Waddoups, Ryan. "Design Within Reach Furnishes Stahl House with 2018 Collection." *Interior Design*, March 16, 2018.
Weber, Greg G. "Appreciation: Jerry Ackerman, California Modern Pioneer." Blog and newsletter, *Design Within Reach: Design Notes*, March 31, 2019.
Weber, Greg G. "Jerome and Evelyn Ackerman: Celebrating a Designing Couple." Catalog, *Design Within Reach*, Winter 2017.
Weiner, Stewart. "A Healthy Restoration." *Palm Springs Life*, February 2015.
Weinstein, David. "Celebrating a Marriage in Art and Life." *CA Modernist*, October 30, 2014.
Weinstein, David. "It Takes Two." *CA Modern*, Spring 2021.
Weinstein, David. "Palm Springs to Celebrate the Ackermans." *Eichler Network*, November 20, 2019.
Weinstein, David. "Partners by Design." *CA Modern*, Summer 2010.
Weinstein, David. "Taking the Plunge." *CA Modern*, Summer 2013.
Williamson, Leslie. *Handcrafted Modern: At Home with Mid-century Designers*. New York: Rizzoli, 2010.
Youngblood, Billie Kolb. "Evelyn and Jerome Ackerman: A Creative Combination in ERA." *West Coast Sourcebook: Interior Previews*, November–December 1963.
Zaki, Haily. "A Q&A with Dan Chavkin: The Ackermans." *Modernism Week*, January 12, 2015.
Zematis, James, Laura Ackerman-Shaw, and Mark Ong. "A Conversation on Jade Snow Wong and Evelyn Ackerman." R & Company, YouTube, December 8, 2022.
Zimbelman, Steven, dir. *The Ackermans: A Marriage of Craft and Design*. With Noah Clark and Station22. Video, Predicta Productions, 2011.

CHRONOLOGY

1920 Jerome Ackerman is born on January 29, in Detroit, Michigan.
1924 Evelyn Lipton (Lipchinsky) is born on January 12, in Detroit, Michigan.
1939 Jerome graduates from Central High School in Detroit and enters Wayne University (now Wayne State University) in Detroit as an art major, is president of the art club, and studies voice, seriously considering a singing career.
1941 Evelyn graduates from Central High School in Detroit and enters the University of Michigan in Ann Arbor, as an art major.
1941 The United States enters World War II. Jerome leaves Wayne at the end of his sophomore year to work as a tool and gauge inspector at a Naval Ordnance plant.
1942 Evelyn's father passes away and she transfers to Wayne University as a fine arts and art history major.
1942 Jerome and Evelyn meet once in the art department at Wayne University.
1945 Evelyn graduates from Wayne University with a BFA (with distinction, fine arts major, art history minor) and is awarded a Wayne University Board of Education Graduate School scholarship.
1945 Jerome completes basic training in Biloxi, MS. He enters the Army Air Corps and serves as a control tower operator at Rhein-Main Air Base, in Frankfurt, Germany.
1947 Jerome, discharged from the military, spends six months in Los Angeles.
1947 Jerome opens a small steel business in Detroit with his cousin.
1948 Evelyn and Jerome meet at Lucé Lipton Interior Design Studio.
1948 Evelyn and Jerome marry on September 12.
1949 Under the GI Bill, Jerome returns to Wayne University to complete his undergraduate degree. He begins showing his ceramics in exhibitions.
1949 *For Modern Living* by Alexander Girard at the Detroit Institute of Arts inspires the Ackermans to pursue careers combining their design and fine arts training.
1949 The Ackermans move into their first apartment in Detroit and purchase furniture at Herman Miller in Grand Rapids, MI.
1949 Evelyn and Jerome visit his family in Los Angeles and meet Beatrice Wood, Gertrud and Otto Natzler, Vivika and Otto Heino, John Follis, and Rex Goode.
1949 The Ackermans become friends with Wilhelm Kåge, director of Gustavsburg pottery, Sweden.
1949 *Wayne University student exhibition*, Detroit, MI.
1950 *Wayne University student exhibition*, Detroit, MI.
1951 *Wayne University student exhibition*, Detroit, MI.
1951 Both graduate from Wayne University, Jerome with a BS (art major) and Art Teaching Certificate, Evelyn with an MFA.
1951 Jerome enters Alfred University's New York College of Ceramics. Evelyn works in the research lab. They become friends with ceramists Ka Kwong Hui, Fong Chow, Val Cushing, Wayne Husted, Herbert Cohen, Robert Turner, Wayne Higby, Karen Karnes, and Robert Weinrib.
1951 Jerome's ceramics are shown in local and national exhibitions.
1951 Jerome works with Marguerite Wildenhain at Alfred University.
1951 *Ceramic National and Traveling Exhibition*, Syracuse Museum (now Everson Museum), Syracuse, NY.
1951 *Michigan State Fair Arts and Crafts Exhibit*, invitational, Detroit, MI.
1951 *Michigan Artist-Craftsman*, Detroit Institute of Arts, Detroit, MI.
1952 Jerome graduates with an MFA in ceramics from Alfred University, NY. He is qualified to teach construction, glazes, materials, models, decoration, and kiln firing.
1952 Evelyn and Jerome move to Los Angeles and establish Jenev Design Studio at 2207 Federal Avenue, Los Angeles, CA.
1952 *Ceramic National and Traveling Exhibition*, Syracuse Museum (now Everson Museum), Syracuse, NY.
1952 *National Decorative Arts and Crafts Exhibition*, Wichita Art Association, Wichita, KS.
1952 *Kiln Club Exhibition of Ceramic Art, Smithsonian Invitational*, Washington, D.C.
1952 *Fiber-Clay-Metal*, St. Paul Art Center (now Minnesota Museum of American Art), St. Paul, MN.
1952 *Michigan State Fair Arts and Crafts Exhibit*, invitational, Detroit, MI.
1953 Jerome develops a group of molded ceramics. To augment their income, they design for Cal Pacific Imports and Evelyn works for comedian Red Skelton.
1953 *Kiln Club Exhibition of Ceramic Art, Smithsonian Invitational*, Washington, D.C.
1953 *Scripps College Invitational*, Claremont, CA.
1953 *Fiber-Clay-Metal*, St. Paul Art Center (now Minnesota Museum of American Art), St. Paul, MN.
1953 *National Decorative Arts and Ceramics Exhibition*, Wichita Art Association, Wichita, KS.
1953 *National Arts and Crafts Competition*, Los Angeles County Fair, third prize, Pomona, CA.
1954 Jerome makes his first sale of Jenev ceramics to Jules Seltzer and Leslie's. Paul McCobb features Jenev ceramics in his Directional Furniture showrooms.
1954 Jerome begins to sell nationally through independent sales representatives.
1954 Jerome's ceramics are shown extensively with F. Carlton Ball, Rupert Deese, Peter Voulkos, and others. Jerome and Voulkos judge ceramics shows together.
1954 *National Decorative Arts and Ceramics Exhibition*, honorable mention, Wichita Art Association, Wichita, KS.
1954 *California Living*, Home Fashion League, Los Angeles, CA.
1954 *Scripps College Invitational*, Claremont, CA.
1954 *Walker Art Center*, Minneapolis, MN.
1954 *California State Fair and Exposition*, Sacramento, CA.
1954 Los Angeles County Fair, *The Arts of Daily Living*, Los Angeles, CA.
1954 Jenev ceramics are featured in *House Beautiful*.
1954 *First National Design Exhibition of Jewelry, Ceramics, Silversmithing, Enameling Invitational*, Texas Western College of the University of Texas, El Paso, TX.
1954 *Young Americans*, second prize, American Craftsmen's Educational Council, America House, New York, NY.
1954 *Annual Festival of the Arts*, first prize, First Unitarian Church, Los Angeles, CA.
1954 University of California, Los Angeles one-man exhibition, Los Angeles, CA.
1954 Los Angeles City College one-man exhibition, Los Angeles, CA.
1954 *Ceramic National and Traveling Exhibition*, Syracuse Museum (now Everson Museum), Syracuse, NY.
1955 *California Designed*, Long Beach Municipal Art Center, Long Beach, CA, and the M. H. de Young Museum, San Francisco, CA.
1955 The Ackermans begin to design and produce mosaic panels and tables.
1955 The J. L. Hudson Company in Detroit features Jenev ceramics and the *Detroit News* publishes the first article on the Michigan natives.
1955 The couple's work begins to appear in the *Los Angeles Times Home* magazine.
1955 Paul Palmer commissions mosaics of Swiss cantons, Mammoth Mountain Inn.
1955 *Scripps College Invitational*, Claremont, CA.
1955 *National Decorative Arts and Ceramics Exhibition*, Wichita Art Association, Wichita, KS.
1955 *California Design I*, Pasadena Art Museum, Pasadena, CA.
1956 The Ackermans introduce silk screens and bas-relief panels to their line.
1956 As members of the American Ceramic Society, the Ackermans join the American Craftsman Council. They become friends with Max and Rita Lawrence of Architectural Pottery, Sam Maloof, Harry McIntosh, Malcolm Leland, and Susan Peterson.
1956 Forming a partnership with architect Sherrill Broudy, Jenev becomes ERA Industrias.
1956 The Ackermans purchase their house in Culver City, CA, from Evelyn's brother.
1956 Evelyn designs the *Fantasy Landscape* mosaic for Sherrill Broudy's apartment building at 11957 Kiowa Avenue, Los Angeles, CA.
1956 *Craftsmanship in a Changing World*, inaugural exhibition, Museum of Contemporary Crafts, New York, NY.
1956 *California Designed*, Long Beach Municipal Art Gallery, Long Beach, CA, and the Oakland Art Museum, Oakland, CA.
1956 *California Design II*, Pasadena Art Museum, Pasadena, CA.
1957 Evelyn's first tapestry design, *Hot Bird*, is handwoven in Mexico.
1957 The Ackermans experiment with a "chem-milling" etching process for aluminum.
1957 Jerome and Evelyn visit mosaic and weaving workshops in Mexico.
1957 Architect Robert Mayer commissions a sculpture for Chandler's shoe store in Pasadena, CA, and anodized aluminum panels for a dress shop in Los Angeles, CA.
1957 Harold Grieve, motion picture art director and interior designer, curates the first Ackerman exhibition at W. & J. Sloane.
1957 *California Design III*, Pasadena Art Museum, Pasadena, CA.
1957 Jerome employs the multiple spindle carving technique to produce wood bas-relief wall panels.
1958 Meeting of the American Ceramic Society, design division, at Bullock's department store includes Jerome and Evelyn Ackerman, Peter Voulkos, Otto and Vivika Heino, David Cressey, Malcolm Leland, Raul Coronel, and Susan Peterson.
1958 Jerome designs porcelain-enameled metal wall and table candleholders.
1958 Evelyn begins designing hand-hooked rugs and wall hangings produced in Japan.
1958 Evelyn designs a mosaic mural, *Sea, Land and Sky*, for an office building by architect Louis Mazzetti at 112 E. Victoria Street, Santa Barbara, CA.
1958 *California Design IV*, Pasadena Art Museum, Pasadena, CA.
1958 *Design in Earth and Fire Design Division*, American Ceramic Society, Bullock's, Los Angeles, CA.
1958 *Crafts West*, Mount St. Mary's College, Los Angeles, CA.
1958 The Ackermans import Pepe Mendoza hardware from Mexico and plastic recessed pulls from Denmark.
1959 The Ackermans import Takana double-warp, reversible weavings from Finland.
1959 *California Design V*, Pasadena Art Museum, Pasadena, CA.
1960 Daughter Laura is born on March 8.
1960 *California Design VI*, Pasadena Art Museum, Pasadena, CA.
1961 To increase design trade exposure, the Ackermans move the ERA

showroom to 8703 Melrose Avenue, Los Angeles, CA. Ceramicist Raul Coronel is across the street.
1961 Interior designer Henry End uses Evelyn's mosaics in the Carlton Towers Hotel, London, and commissions designs for hotels in Aruba and Bermuda.
1961 *California Design VII*, Pasadena Art Museum, Pasadena, CA.
1962 *California Design VIII*, Pasadena Art Museum, Pasadena, CA (triennials follow).
1963 ERA Industrias becomes ERA Industries.
1963 With former business partner Sherrill Broudy, the Ackermans form Panelcarve. Evelyn designs *Ucello*, the first modular carved wood panels for architectural applications.
1963 The Ackermans are featured in *West Coast Sourcebook: Interior Previews*.
1963 At Isomata, the USC art camp in Idyllwild, CA, Evelyn learns how to make puppets from Harry Barnett of the Yale Puppeteers.
1963 The Ackermans add traditional Aubusson woven tapestries with medieval themes from France and Germany.
1964 ERA outgrows the showroom on Melrose Avenue and moves to 8817 Beverly Boulevard, Los Angeles, CA.
1964 Evelyn makes finger puppet kits as a fund raiser for their daughter's nursery school that are later marketed through ERA.
1964 The Ackermans import papier mâché sculptural figures from Mexico.
1964 Evelyn designs Hydrastone wall plaques, bookends, and sculptures.
1964 *World's Fair Pavilion of American Interiors*, New York, NY.
1965 Jerome designs *Antico* hand-cast brass hardware produced in Italy.
1965 *California Design IX*, Pasadena Art Museum, Pasadena, CA.
1968 Evelyn enrolls in enameling and jewelry making classes.
1968 Artist-in-charge, Evelyn creates 12 needlepoint hangings for Litton Industries corporate offices in Beverly Hills, CA, commissioned by Saphier, Lerner, Schindler.
1968 *California Design X*, Pasadena Art Museum, Pasadena, CA.
1971 The Alan Ladd Building, Palm Springs, CA, by architect Hugh Kaptur featuring *Ucello* doors and transom, appears on the cover of *American Journal of Building Design*.
1971 *California Design XI*, Pasadena Art Museum, Pasadena, CA.
1973 Jerome adapts Evelyn's small carved wood plaques for practical applications.
1973 Charles Luckman Associates commissions *Morning Dove* and *Aerial View* silk screens for the Hyatt Hotel, Broadway Plaza, Los Angeles, CA.
1973 A set of large hand-hooked hangings are commissioned for Don Koll office buildings in Newport Beach, CA, by architects Langdon & Wilson.
1976 *California Design '76: A Bicentennial Celebration*, Pacific Design Center, Los Angeles, CA.
1979 The Ackermans, with Forms+Surfaces, move their showroom to the Pacific Design Center contract floor, across from their previous Melrose showroom.
1979 Evelyn designs carved oak doors for Congregation Ahavas Israel, Grand Rapids, MI, in memory of her twin sister, Roslyn.
1980 The Ackermans discontinue developing new ERA products and move into a converted warehouse. Jerome continues to sell to architects and interior designers.
1984 *Stories from the Bible*, cloisonné series, acquired by the Renwick Gallery, Smithsonian American Art Museum, Washington, D.C.
1984 At the Los Angeles County Museum of Art, Evelyn volunteers as a researcher in the Costume and Textile department.
1990 Jerome, semi-retired, resumes hand-throwing and casting Jenev pieces, participates in numerous Southern California exhibitions, and sells in galleries.
1990 Evelyn, a renowned expert on antique dolls, dollhouses, and toys, writes hundreds of articles and publishes five books over the next two decades.
1994 *A Secret History of Design in Los Angeles*, Pacific Design Center, Los Angeles, CA.
1997 *Skilled Work: American Craft in the Renwick Gallery*, National Museum of American Art, Smithsonian Institution, Washington, D.C.
1998 *A Quintessential Functional, Ritual, and Metaphorical Vessel Show*, Earthen Art Works, Los Angeles, CA.
1998 *Featured Artist: Jerome Ackerman*, Del Mano Gallery, Brentwood, CA.
1998 *L.A. Modern and Beyond*, Los Angeles County Museum of Art, Pacific Design Center, Los Angeles, CA.
1998 *California Landscapes and Earthshapes*, Millard Sheets Gallery, Pomona, CA.
2000 *Made in California: Art, Image and Identity, 1900–2000*, Los Angeles County Museum of Art, Los Angeles, CA.
2000 *Color and Fire: Defining Moments in Studio Ceramics, 1950–2000*, Los Angeles County Museum of Art, Los Angeles, CA.
2001 *California Pottery: Mission to Modernism*, San Francisco Museum of Modern Art, San Francisco, CA.
2003 *California Pottery: Mission to Modernism*, Autry Museum, Los Angeles, CA.
2003 *California Design*, R 20th Century Gallery, Paris, France.
2004 *Ink & Clay 30*, Kellogg University Art Gallery, California Polytechnic University, Pomona, CA.
2004 *Envisioning Jacob's Ladder: Religion, Representation and Allusion in American Visual Culture 1750–2000*, Iris and B. Gerald Cantor Gallery, Holy Cross College, Worcester, MA.
2004 *Celebrating Nature*, Craft and Folk Art Museum, Los Angeles, CA.
2004 *Clay and California*, Free Hand Gallery, Los Angeles, CA.
2005 *California Design*, Reform Gallery, Los Angeles, CA.
2007 *Craft in America*, Virtual Exhibition.
2008 Museum of California Design Henry Award.
2008 *Mythical Creatures and Characters*, Craft and Folk Art Museum, Los Angeles, CA.
2009 *Masters of Mid-Century California Modernism: Evelyn and Jerome Ackerman*, Mingei International Museum, San Diego, CA.
2009 *Evelyn and Jerome Ackerman*, Modernism Week, Palm Springs, CA.
2010 Wayne State University Distinguished Alumni Award.
2010 Alfred University Alumni Award for Distinguished Achievement.
2010 *Handcrafted Modern* with Ackerman, Bertoia, Blunk, Eames, Frey, Gropius, Esherick, Harper, Kagan, Kapel, Nakashima, Risom, Wright, and Zeisel.
2011 *Pacific Standard Time Art in L.A. 1945–1980* sponsored by the Getty.
2011 *A Marriage of Craft and Design: The Work of Evelyn and Jerome Ackerman*, Craft and Folk Art Museum, Los Angeles, CA.
2011 *California Design, 1930–1965: Living in a Modern Way*, Los Angeles County Museum of Art, Los Angeles, CA. Travels to the National Art Center, Tokyo, Japan, Auckland Art Gallery, Auckland, New Zealand, Queensland Art Gallery, Brisbane, Australia, and Peabody Essex Museum, Salem, MA.
2011 *Common Ground: Ceramics in Southern California 1945–1975*, American Museum of Ceramic Art, Pomona, CA.
2011 *Golden State of Craft: California 1960–1985*, Craft and Folk Art Museum, Los Angeles, CA.
2012 *California's Designing Women, 1896–1986*, Autry National Center, Los Angeles, CA.
2012 Evelyn passes away on November 28 at age 88.
2013 Los Angeles Conservancy Modern Committee Modern Masters Award.
2014 *Hand-in-Hand: Ceramics, Mosaics, Tapestries, and Woodcarvings by the California Mid-Century Designers Evelyn and Jerome Ackerman* by Dan Chavkin and Lisa Thackaberry.
2015 *Masters of Midcentury California Design: The Story of Evelyn and Jerome Ackerman*, Modernism Week, Palm Springs, CA.
2015 Film, *In Tandem: The Life and Work of Jerry and Evelyn Ackerman.*
2015 Daughter Laura establishes Ackerman Modern.
2017 *AMOCA A to Z: AMOCA's Permanent Collection*, American Museum of Ceramic Art, Pomona, CA.
2017 *Frank Brothers: The Store That Modernized Modern*, California State University Long Beach, Long Beach, CA.
2017 *Found in Translation: Design in California and Mexico, 1915–1985*, Los Angeles County Museum of Art, Los Angeles, CA.
2017 Design Within Reach reissues an exclusive collection of Jenev ceramics.
2018 *Living with Clay: California Ceramics Collections*, California State University Fullerton, Fullerton, CA.
2018 *Discovering Saar Ceramics*, American Museum of Ceramic Art, Pomona, CA.
2019 *In Tandem*, Modern Phoenix Week, Phoenix, AZ.
2019 Jerome passes away on March 31 at age 99.
2019 *Thread*, Long Beach Art Museum, Long Beach, CA.
2019 *California Cool: Mid-Century Modernism on the Central Coast*, Museum of Ventura County, Ventura, CA.
2020 *Partners in Design*, Modernism Week, Palm Springs, CA.
2020 *CA Designed 1955*, Long Beach Art Museum, Long Beach, CA.
2020 *Decade by Decade: Women Artists of California*, Long Beach Art Museum, Long Beach, CA.
2020 Evelyn and Jerome Ackerman Endowed Scholarship, Wayne State University, and Jerome Ackerman Endowed Internship, Alfred Ceramic Art Museum, established.
2022 *Born Too Tall: California Women Designers, Postwar to Postmodern*, R & Company, New York, NY.
2022 UCLA Faculty Center and large installation of Castles Panelcarve renovated.
2023 Retailer CB2 releases an Ackerman "Design Legends" collection.
2024 *Evelyn Ackerman: The Collection of Gary and Laura Maurer*, R & Company, New York, NY.
2025 Docomomo, Goldstein Museum of Design and Textile Center, Minneapolis, MN.
2025 *Piece by Piece: Evelyn and Jerome Ackerman Mosaics*, R & Company, New York, NY.
2025 *Eventually Everything Connects: Mid-Century Modern Design in the US*, Cranbrook Art Museum, Bloomfield Hills, MI.
2025 *Material Curiosity by Design: Evelyn and Jerome Ackerman, Midcentury to Today*, Craft Contemporary, Los Angeles, CA.

INDEX

PHOTOGRAPHY CREDITS

Every effort has been made to locate copyright holders. Any omissions will be corrected in future printings.

Evelyn Ackerman: 28–29, 51. Jerome Ackerman: 23, 48, 54, 63, 103. Laura Ackerman-Shaw: 120, 124–125. Alderfer Auction: 168. Mark April/J3Productions.com: 248–249. Bonhams: 148. CBS. Photo still from *The Twilight Zone* courtesy of CBS Broadcasting, Inc.: 184–185. California Design Collection, Oakland Museum of California. Courtesy of the Oakland Museum of California: 212–213. Christopher Burke Studios: 183. Dan Chavkin: cover, 4, 8, 10–11, 12–13, 19, 20, 21, 24, 31, 32, 36, 46–47, 68, 70–71, 72–73, 74–75 bottom, 76 left, 79, 80 top row, 2nd row left, 3rd row right, bottom row right, 81, 84, 85, 86–87, 90–91, 92, 93, 94–95, 96–97, 98, 100, 102, 104–105, 106, 108–109 bottom, 114–115, 117 left, 122–123, 125 right, 128, 130, 132, 133, 134–135, 136, 137, 138–139, 140, 141, 143, 144, 145, 147, 152, 153, 154, 155, 156, 157, 158, 159, 161, 162–163, 164–165, 166, 169, 170–171, 174, 176, 177, 179, 180, 181, 186–187, 188, 189, 190–191, 192, 194–195, 196–197, 198, 200, 201, 202, 203, 204, 205, 206, 209, 210, 211, 214–215, 216, 220, 223, 226, 227, 228–229, 230–231, 233, 234, 236–237, 239, 242, 243, 245, 246–247. Rose Greenberg Ackerman: 14–15. Heritage Auctions/HA.com: 116 left. Leonard Auction: 80 bottom row center. Milton Lipton: 6–7, 26–27, 44, 88–89. Bob Lopez: 16, 60, 219. Los Angeles County Museum of Art, Collection of Jerome Ackerman. Photo © Museum Associates/LACMA: 150. R & Company/Logan Jackson: 80 bottom row left, 112–113 bottom, 119 left, 126, 127, 146, 193. Private collection, courtesy of R & Company. Photograph by Logan Jackson. Rago/Wright/LAMA: 2–3, 76 right, 82, 108–109 top, 110–111, 112–113 top, 116 right, 118, 119 right, 121, 142, 172–173. Juan Salazar and Luis Corona: 117 right. Julius Shulman © J. Paul Getty Trust. Getty Research Institute, Los Angeles (2004. R. 10): 107, 235. Dorothy Siegel: opposite half-title page. Smithsonian American Art Museum: 240. Evelyn Ackerman, *Stories from the Bible*, 1984-1985, cloisonne enamel with silver wire on copper, each: 3 ⅛ x 3 ⅛ x ⅛ in. (8.0 x 8.0 x .3 cm), Smithsonian American Art Museum, Gift of Laura Ackerman-Shaw in honor of her mother Evelyn Ackerman, 1996.53A-NN, © 1985, Evelyn Ackerman: 240. Jerome Ackerman, *Monks*, 1994, stoneware with matte and semi-matte glazes, 8 ¼ x 8 ⅝ in. (21.0 x 22.0 cm) diam., Smithsonian American Art Museum, Gift of the artist, 1996.76.1, © 1994, Jerome Ackerman: 244. Ackerman Archives: 33, 34, 37, 38, 40–41, 42, 43, 52–53, 56–57, 58–59, 62, 64–65, 66–67, 74 top, 77, 78, 80 2nd row center and right, 3rd row left and center, 99, 131, 149, 151, 160, 167, 178, 182, 208, 217, 218, 222, 224–225, 232, 238. Thank you to Andrew French for photographing the ephemera in the Ackerman Archives.

CONTRIBUTORS

Laura Ackerman-Shaw, the daughter of Jerome and Evelyn Ackerman, received B.A. and M.A. degrees in English literature with honors from Stanford University. After 35 years in publishing as a director of design, editorial, production, and translations, she established Ackerman Modern. Laura stewards her parents' design legacy through exhibitions, publications, and licensing. She has written widely and serves on a Manitoga / Russell Wright Design Center advisory board. In 2020 Laura endowed the Evelyn and Jerome Ackerman Scholarship at Wayne State University and the Jerome Ackerman Internship at the Alfred Ceramic Art Museum for art students.

Glenn Adamson is a curator, writer, and historian based in New York and London. Previously director of the Museum of Arts and Design and Head of Research at the Victoria and Albert Museum, he is Design Doha artistic director and Design Miami 2024 curatorial director. His publications include *Thinking Through Craft* (2007), *The Craft Reader* (2010), *Postmodernism: Style and Subversion* (2011, with Jane Pavitt), *The Invention of Craft* (2013), *Art in the Making* (2016, with Julia Bryan-Wilson), *Fewer Better Things: The Hidden Wisdom of Objects* (2018), *Objects: USA 2020* and *Craft: An American History* (2021), *A Century of Tomorrows: How Imagining the Future Shapes the Present* (2024), and *Nike: Form Follows Motion* (2024, editor).

Danielle Charlap is a Los Angeles-based curator and art historian focused on the intersection of design, craft, and everyday life. She has worked on a wide range of curatorial projects over the last 15 years, including *Scandinavian Design and the United States, 1890–1980*, Los Angeles County Museum of Art (2022–2023), and is the curator of the 2025–2026 Ackerman exhibition *Material Curiosity by Design: Evelyn and Jerome Ackerman, Midcentury to Today* at Craft Contemporary, Los Angeles. She is completing her PhD at the University of Southern California and received an M.A. from the Bard Graduate Center and a B.A. from Harvard University.

Dan Chavkin studied at the Art Center College of Design in Pasadena, California. Upon graduating, he moved to New York, and began his career shooting celebrities for top magazines. Dan collects midcentury furniture and vintage film posters and periodicals. In 2014, Dan co-authored with Lisa Thackaberry *Hand-In-Hand*, the first book about Evelyn and Jerome Ackerman. A midcentury modern architecture photography specialist, Dan published *Unseen Midcentury Desert Modern* in 2016 and *Star Trek: Designing the Final Frontier* in 2021. Dan co-authored *Architectural Pottery: Ceramics for a Modern Landscape*, in 2024.

Dale Carolyn Gluckman, former head of the department of Costumes and Textiles at Los Angeles County Museum of Art (LACMA) has been an independent curator and museum consultant since 2005. She has published widely and organized many exhibitions, including the award-winning *When Art Became Fashion: Kosode in Edo-Period Japan*. With Jo Lauria, she co-curated the first Ackerman retrospective, *Masters of Mid-Century California Modernism* (Mingei International, San Diego, 2009). In 2011 it traveled as *A Marriage of Craft and Design* to CAFAM (now Craft Contemporary), Los Angeles. Dale was a lead consultant in creating the Queen Sirikit Museum of Textiles, Bangkok, Thailand.

Jeffrey Head writes about art, architecture, and design. He is the author of *Paul Evans: Designer & Sculptor, No Nails, No Lumber—The Bubble Houses of Wallace Neff, Regional Landscape Architecture: Southern California, Mediterranean Modern* and *Regional Landscape Architecture: Northern California, Rooted in Resilience*. Recently, Jeffrey co-authored *Architectural Pottery: Ceramics for a Modern Landscape*. He coedited the museum catalog *Jack Rogers Hopkins: California Design Maverick* and contributed essays for *Modern Americana: Studio Furniture from High Craft to High Glam, Lustron Stories,* and *Craig Ellwood: Self-Made Modern*.

David A. Keeps is a Detroit-born, Los Angeles-based writer, editor, and ceramic artist who has contributed to *Architectural Digest Pro, Elle Decor, House Beautiful, Travel + Leisure, Los Angeles Times*, and 1stDibs' *Introspective*. He made his television host debut in *Art & the City*, a travel show that was the first series from Ovation in 2007. David has written and produced television shows for Bravo and the Esquire Network.

Jo Lauria is a Los Angeles-based curator, educator, and award winning author. Her forward-thinking advocacy for the handmade has been rewarded with a lifetime of acclaimed projects. She is adjunct curator of the American Museum of Ceramic Art (AMOCA) and faculty member at Otis College of Art and Design. With Dale Gluckman, she co-curated the Ackermans' first retrospective, *Masters of Mid-Century California Modernism* (Mingei International, San Diego, 2009). It traveled to the Craft and Folk Art Museum, Los Angeles, as *A Marriage of Craft and Design* (2011). Her most recent exhibition and book premiered in 2024 at AMOCA: *Architectural Pottery, Ceramics for a Modern Landscape*.

CAPTIONS

COVER AND BACK COVER A striking combination of art and craft, the *Horse* pull, designed in 1959, shimmers in hand-cast polished brass and inlaid turquoise.

OPPOSITE HALF TITLE PAGE Jerry and Evelyn Ackerman posed for a formal portrait in 1949.

PAGES 2–3 A detail of the vibrant mosaic tiles in the iconic *Elipses* reveals the overlapping rhythm of colors and pattern.

PAGE 4 The cheerful blue and yellow 1968 *Striped Candy Tree*, 26 by 46 inches, was handwoven in Mexico.

PAGES 6-7 Jerry worked at the wheel while Evelyn finished a ceramic in the Jenev studio at 2207 Federal Avenue in Los Angeles.

OPPOSITE CONTENTS A soft, stoney matte glaze and a persimmon and black trim accent the intricately carved geometric pattern on Jerry's 1993 stoneware covered jar.

PAGES 10–11 Jerry's *Autumn Abstract* design, measuring 54 by 24 inches, shows the quality of the hooking. The overlapping abstract shapes and colors merged in the intersecting patterns were inspired by the letter "H."

PAGES 12–13 A detail from *Riders*, a 9-by-39-inch woodcarving, was part of a group created in 1963 with stylized heraldic themes that included *Warriors* and *Arches*. Like many of Evelyn's designs, it coordinated with both traditional and contemporary decor.

PAGES 14–15 Evelyn and Jerry relaxed on the beach in Frankfort, Michigan, in the summer of 1949.

PAGES 250–251 Evelyn and Jerry attended the 2009 opening of the first retrospective of their work, *Masters of Mid-Century California Modernism*, at the Mingei International Museum in San Diego, California. Evelyn made her silver pendant at Wayne University in 1942, cutting the abstract figure with a jigsaw because she did not know how to solder.

ACKNOWLEDGMENTS

This book would not exist were it not for an email that I received in 2012 from Dan Chavkin, inquiring about publishing a book on my parents. I learned that he was a respected mid-century architectural photographer. My Dad and I took a leap of faith and said yes. Dan was enamored with my parents' designs, and along the way, fell in love with them as people. Fortunately Dan's photography also graces this new book. Lisa Thackaberry, who joined Dan in the efforts to bring a book to fruition, quickly became part of the team and provided invaluable insights and guidance. A decade has passed since the publication of *Hand-in-Hand: Ceramics, Mosaics, Tapestries, and Woodcarvings by the California Mid-Century Designers Evelyn and Jerome Ackerman.* Dan and Lisa have my heartfelt gratitude for passing the torch, their unwavering support, and insighful input.

Creating this book has been an unexpected but treasured experience, and I am deeply grateful to the many people who have cheered and supported it along the way.

I am exceptionally indebted to Suzanne Slesin, Frederico Farina, and Julian Cosma at Pointed Leaf Press, who had the vision to publish the first book about my parents and enthusiastically embraced the opportunity to create a new publication. Their passion for my parents' designs, understanding of the work, and sensitivity to the content is reflected in these pages. They have been dedicated partners in making this book what it is.

Without the generous support from the following individuals and organizations, I could not have completed this project. Trina Turk, Gary and Laura Maurer, Rago/Wright/Los Angeles Modern Auctions, Gary and Joan Gand, Richard and Alice Kulka, Jonathan Adler, Billings Auction, Heritage Auctions, David Shinder, Jenny Cottle, Eames Office, Palm Springs Modern Committee, Eames Demetrios and Shelley Mills, Rodney and Cindra Stolk, Gary L. Johns, Lou and Amy Zucaro, Bonnie Ruttan, Randi Merel and Allen LeHew.

I am indebted to the photographers, galleries, auction houses, curators, archivists, museums, collectors, and media who provided works or photography. Dan Chavkin, Logan Jackson, Christopher Burke, Andrew French, Peter Murray at CBS, Carole Ita White, James Zematis at R & Company, Gerard O'Brien at Reform gallery, Steve Aldana at Esoteric Survey, Jeff Schuerholz at Fat Chance, Emilie Sims, Jamie Shi, and Kyra Rooney at Rago/Wright/Los Angeles Modern Auctions, Ed Beardsley at Heritage Auctions, John Leonard at Leonard Auction, Ranae Gabel at Alderfer Auction, Rich Carmichael at Billings Auction, Jason Stein at Bonhams, Richard Sorensen at Smithsonian American Art Museum, Piper Severance at Los Angeles County Museum of Art, Virginia Mokslaveskas at Getty Research Institute, Emily Smith at Oakland Museum of California, Jonathan Lo and Mark April at J3 Productions, Aditi Mehha at After Shoot, Juan Salazar and Luis Corona, Gary and Laura Maurer, and Eileen Kleiman and Peter Luyre.

To the contributors—Glenn Adamson, Danielle Charlap, Dale Carolyn Gluckman, Jeffrey Head, David Keeps, and Jo Lauria—whose expertise and scholarship coupled with a deep affection for and understanding of my parents and their designs informed their writing, thank you for your invaluable insights, eloquent text, collaborative contributions, and enduring friendship.

Special thanks to Rody Lopez, Executive Director of Craft Contemporary, for his support of a new Ackerman exhibit and this project, and to Danielle Charlap, exhibition curator, whose conceptualization for *Material Curiosity by Design* inspired a few of this book's photo spreads.

I am immensely grateful to curators Dale Carolyn Gluckman and Jo Lauria, who met my mother at the Los Angeles County Museum of Art's Costume and Textile department when she was a volunteer researcher. Their vision brought to life the first retrospective of my parents' designs, *Masters of Mid-Century California Modernism* at the Mingei Museum in San Diego in 2009–2010.

For shining a spotlight my parents' work on the East Coast, thank you James Zematis, Evan Snyderman, Zesty Meyers, and Grace Londono at R & Company, New York.

To those who have shared the Ackerman story in other ways, especially the filmmakers Katie Nartonis and Margaret Halkin and Amber Asay of Women Designers You Should Know, thank you.

Thanks to Liz Waytkus, Executive Director of Docomomo US, for highlighting my parents' accomplishments and encouraging me to expand my article for this book.

To the devoted collectors of my parents' work and those who have family pieces, your enthusiasm keeps their spirit alive.

Special thanks to CB2, its design and development team in particular, for collaborating with me to share my parents' story and bring their designs to a new audience.

I extend my sincere appreciation to Ted Max and Ed Komen for their guidance, Sandra Rosenbaum for her early research, and Jonathan Lo and Paul Choi for their web expertise.

To my husband, Marc, for his tireless work helping me gather my parents' 60 years of archived materials and nearly inexhaustible patience with my absorption in this project, and to our son, Aaron, and daughter-in-law, Kristen, for their support and encouragement, all my love.

Finally, and most importantly, to my parents, Evelyn and Jerry, whose design legacy endures and whose love was the best gift of all. It is to them that this book is dedicated.

—Laura Ackerman-Shaw, January 2025

PUBLISHER Suzanne Slesin
CREATIVE DIRECTOR Frederico Farina
EDITORIAL ASSISTANT Julian Cosma
COPY EDITOR Amelia Kutschbach
ISBN 978-1-938461-66-8 L.O.C. 2024926790
First Edition | Printed in Spain

Pointed Leaf Press, LLC., 136 Baxter Street, Suite 1C, New York, NY 10013.

“Not many marriage
people working tog
we have, who are r
terms of approache
and artistic bent. T
able to stay togethe
side by side and pr
felt was an endurin
made us happy.”—